D1164931

GRAY
MATTER

Learning and Memory

GRAY
MATTER

GRAY
MATTER

Learning and Memory

Andy Hudmon

Yale University

Department of Neurology

CHELSEA HOUSE
P U B L I S H E R S

A Haights Cross Communications ✦ Company ®

Philadelphia

CHELSEA HOUSE PUBLISHERS

VP, NEW PRODUCT DEVELOPMENT Sally Cheney
DIRECTOR OF PRODUCTION Kim Shinners
CREATIVE MANAGER Takeshi Takahashi
MANUFACTURING MANAGER Diann Grasse
PRODUCTION EDITOR Noelle Nardone
PHOTO EDITOR Sarah Bloom

STAFF FOR LEARNING AND MEMORY

PROJECT MANAGEMENT Dovetail Content Solutions
DEVELOPMENTAL EDITOR Carol Field
PROJECT MANAGER Pat Mrozek
ART DIRECTOR Carol Bleistine
SERIES AND COVER DESIGNER Terry Mallon
LAYOUT Maryland Composition Company, Inc.

A Haights Cross Communications ◢ Company ®

www.chelseahouse.com

First Printing

10 9 8 7 6 5 4 3 2 1

Library of Congress Cataloging-in-Publication Data

Hudmon, Andrew.
    Learning and memory / Andrew Hudmon.
    p. cm. — (Gray matter)
Includes bibliographical references and index.
    ISBN 0-7910-8638-0
1. Learning. 2. Memory. 3. Neuropsychology. I. Title. II. Series.
QP408.H83 2005
612.8′2—dc22   2005011699

Contents

1 The Neuroanatomy of Learning and Memory

THE BRAIN AS AN ORGAN

Imagine what your life would be like if you had no ability to remember or learn. Imagine starting each day without having the benefit of the successes and failures of the previous day. Or the day before. Or *any* day before. Without learning or memory, the most mundane tasks would become complex problems. For most people, the inability to distinguish family, friends, and strangers would be a frightening prospect, but for people who have profound deficits in their ability to learn new experiences, this can be a reality. Later in this book, we discuss brain trauma and disease and the effects they can have on brain function. We also look at studies involving experimental brain surgery, which have shown that a dysfunction of learning and memory developed late in life does not necessarily produce identifiable deficits in a person's ability to recall the past or perform day-to-day activities, such as reading, writing, and having a coherent conversation. Probe deeper, however, and remarkable tales are revealed— tales, for example, of individuals who have a lifetime of memories but a complete inability to form new ones. Without learning and memory, we lose the capacity to acquire new facts, faces, and places. Some individuals with dysfunctional learning and memory are by all accounts, frozen in time, starting each day fresh, with no recollection of any activities or experiences from the previous day. In this chapter, we examine the basic organization and function of the nervous system, while carefully navigating the terminology that is essential to understanding the fundamental concepts of the neurobiology of learning and memory.

THE BRAIN AS PART OF THE NERVOUS SYSTEM

One fundamental tenet of neuroscience is that the ability to store and recall the memory of a new experience to shape behavior is a direct reflection of brain function. Just as your heart is the organ designed to pump blood, the brain is the organ designed to learn and remember. It is the repository for all of the pieces that make you who you are (faces, places, motor skills, and past and present events, just to list a few examples).

Brain Size and Intelligence

Brain size varies dramatically among vertebrates. Brain size does not always correlate with body size; however, as a general rule, the bigger the animal, the bigger the brain. For example, a sperm whale's brain and an elephant's brain are roughly 4 to 5 times the mass of a human's brain. Are sperm whales and elephants more intelligent than humans simply because their brains are bigger? It is difficult to draw conclusions regarding brain size and cognitive capacity, as a bigger body requires a larger brain to control the larger muscles. Perhaps a better index would be to compare the relative ratio of brain to body size. An average human brain is roughly 2% of its body weight for a 150-pound (60-kg) man, whereas the ratio of brain to body size for sperm whales (assuming they weigh 15,000 kg) and elephants (assuming a weight of 6,000 kg) varies from 0.05–0.1%, respectively. This suggests that, for our size, humans possess a rather large brain. Does the fact that dolphins and chimpanzees,

The nervous system is composed of the **central nervous system (CNS)** and the **peripheral nervous system (PNS)**. The CNS, which includes the brain and spinal cord, is responsible for coordinating the body's adjustments and reactions to both external and internal conditions. The PNS consists of all the nerves that connect the CNS with the rest of the body—the organs, sense organs, muscles, blood vessels, and glands. The PNS provides **autonomic** (automatic) control of internal organs and sensory information about muscle and limb (e.g., arm and leg) position. It is also responsible for keeping the CNS informed about the environment, a function it performs through the senses (e.g., touch, pain, heat, and cold), as well as relaying motor (movement) commands from the CNS to the muscle.

which have relative brain to body size ratios of 0.6–0.8%, make these animals as intelligent as humans? What criteria would you use to compare the intelligence of each of these species? Neither dolphins nor whales use tools or drive cars; however, humans cannot navigate the open ocean without a compass and celestial readings. In general, mammals do have larger and more complex brains than other vertebrates.

Organism	Brain weight	Body weight
Human	1,400 g	62,000 g
Chimp	420 g	68,000 g
Monkey	140 g	30,000 g
Cat	30 g	3,300 g
Rabbit	12 g	2,500 g
Bird	1 g	113 g
Frog	0.1g	18 g

g = gram

A comparison of animal brains

The functional unit of the nervous system is the **neuron**. Neurons vary greatly in their shape and size; however, the unifying characteristic of all neurons (whether they come from the PNS or CNS, or from a worm or human being) is their ability to send and receive information. This ability to communicate information is achieved through a process called **neurotransmission**, which is a form of signaling that uses specialized biochemicals.

ANATOMY OF THE BRAIN

The most obvious structural features of the brain include:

1. Two large lobes that appear symmetrical and divide the brain in half.
2. Intricate folds or grooves that decorate the brain's outer surface.
3. A stalk that protrudes from the back of the brain.

These basic characteristics are evident in the brains of all animals.

The human brain is a striking sight (Figure 1.1). The average adult human brain weighs about 1,400 grams (3 pounds) and is roughly 16.7 cm (6.57 inches) long, 14 cm (5.5 inches) wide, and 9.3 cm (3.66 inches) high. It is light gray to pink on the outside and has the consistency of a water balloon. The brain sits protected within the skull in a viscous fluid (**cerebrospinal fluid**) that acts as a shock absorber to protect the brain from physical trauma and sudden changes in motion.

Like all of the brains in the animal kingdom, the human brain is divided into two halves: the right and left **cerebral hemispheres**. The surface of the cerebral hemispheres is called the **cerebral cortex**, which is composed of four lobes named after the overlying bones of the skull: frontal, parietal, occipital, and temporal.

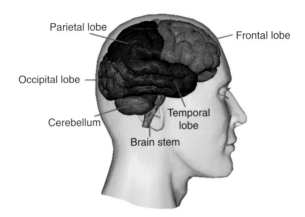

Figure 1.1 This diagram of the human brain shows the four main divisions of the brain: the frontal lobe (purple), the parietal lobe (red), the temporal lobe (blue), and the occipital lobe (green). The cerebellum (pink; primarily used for voluntary muscle movements) and brain stem (orange; involved in arousal, attention, and consciousness) are also pictured.

Studies of patients with brain trauma have revealed a lot about the functions and attributes of each cortical lobe. The **frontal lobe** functions primarily to control movement and to plan for the future. In addition to being the brain's emotion control center, the frontal lobe is instrumental to personality. The **parietal lobe** is involved mainly with the senses and perception. It also provides the spatial representation of the world around us, such as the ability to determine left and right and to perceive objects. The parietal lobe is responsible for integrating sensory information into a single perception (cognition); when it is damaged, it can cause difficulty with writing, mathematics, and language. The **occipital lobe** functions as the center for visual cognition, including information related to color and movement. The **temporal lobe** has many functions. It contains two structures that are important to behavior and memory formation: the amygdala and the hippocampus. The almond-shaped **amygdala** is located toward the front of the temporal lobe and plays a role in motivation and emotional behavior.

The **hippocampus** is a seahorse-shaped structure connected to the amygdala that is important to emotions, motivation, learning, and short-term and long-term memory formation. Damage to the temporal lobe may be associated with deficits in auditory and visual processing, impaired language skills and verbal reasoning, problems with long-term memory, altered personality, or aberrant behavior.

The amygdala and hippocampus make up part of what is called the **limbic system**, a group of brain structures that are essential to learning and memory. Other key structures of the limbic system are the **thalamus** and **hypothalamus**. The thalamus is located in the center of the brain and is responsible for the recognition of sensory stimuli (with the exception of smell) and the relay of sensory impulses to the cerebral cortex. The hypothalamus, located immediately below the thalamus and roughly the size of a pea, is involved in autonomic processes such as temperature regulation, food intake, and emotional activity, and is believed to be important in controlling sleep and wakefulness. The function of the limbic system is discussed in more detail in Chapter 5.

The grooves on the surface of the brain are infoldings and convolutions of the cerebral cortex. The crests of these folds are called **gyri** (singular is *gyrus*) and the intervening grooves are called **sulci** (singular is *sulcus*). Gyri and sulci maintain a relative position from brain to brain, which has led to each sulcus and gyrus being named. For example, the central sulcus separates the precentral gyrus (devoted to motor function) and the postcentral gyrus (concerned with sensory function). If a neurosurgeon inserted electrodes on the motor side of the central sulcus, the patient would exhibit muscle movement, whereas stimulation of the sensory side would elicit sensations. Each lobe of the brain has specific landmarks in the form of gyri and sulci that demark their respective territories. For example, the central sulcus delineates the frontal and parietal lobes. The smaller convolutions that reside within the major gyri and sulci have unique folds that produce a fingerprint-like unique pattern on the surface of each person's brain.

The presence of gyri and sulci serve to increase the surface area of the brain. If you could flatten the folds of the human brain into one large surface, it would occupy roughly one to two pages of a newspaper! Why is increasing the surface area of the brain important? Maximizing the surface area of the brain produces a larger volume that can be used to squeeze a greater number of neurons into the limited space of the skull. The neurons are the functional units of the brain. The brain should not be viewed as a random collection of 100 billion neurons, but rather distinct subsystems that are formed by functionally related neurons, termed **neuronal networks**. It is the collective power of these neuronal networks that enable the brain to perform its many, varied functions—from regulating muscle control, to processing sensory information, to conducting all of the cognitive activities that make you who you are (see "Functional Magnetic Resonance Imaging" box).

■ **Learn more about the topography and function of the human brain** Search the Internet for *brain structure* or *brain function.*

ANATOMY OF A NEURON

The function of a neuron is to receive information (from the environment or from other neurons), process it, and then pass it along to **excitable** cells (cells that can respond to the information by generating an appropriate action—neurons and muscle cells are two examples). Through fast (electrical) and slow (chemical) communication, neurons process, propagate, and store information. Although there may be more than 10,000 different types of neurons in the CNS, all neurons can be classified into one of three main categories based on their function:

Functional Magnetic Resonance Imaging

Advances in imaging technology, such as magnetic resonance imaging (MRI), have permitted researchers to noninvasively collect real-time images of changes in neuronal activity. In the brain, active neurons require increased blood flow to meet metabolic demands, a process that an MRI detector reads as enhanced oxygen levels. MRI used to assess biological function (or neuronal activity while doing certain tasks) is called functional magnetic resonance imaging (fMRI). A typical fMRI study takes up to 3 hours and is extremely computer intensive, as thousands of high-resolution images must be aligned and corrected for subtle changes in head position. The area of activity is typically depicted as an area of bright color (usually yellow to red) superimposed over a gray background. fMRI has produced significant advances in a relatively new interdisciplinary approach called cognitive neuroscience, which is aimed at the development of mind and brain research to understand the psychological, computational, and neuroscientific basis of cognition. In the fMRI shown in this illustration, the test subject has just received a squirt of orange juice, which is represented in the brain as a bright orange and yellow area of activity.

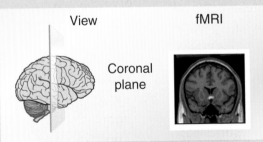

View   fMRI

Coronal
plane

Cross-section of the human brain

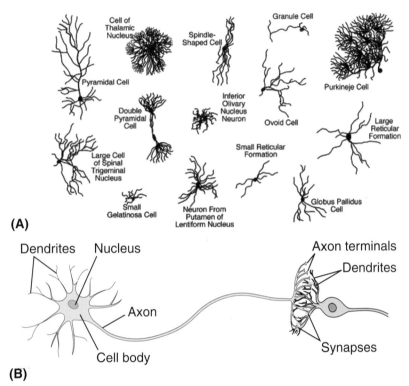

(A)

(B)

Figure 1.2 There are many kinds of neurons in the central nervous system. Diagram A shows different types of neurons, based on the drawings of Spanish physician Santiago Ramòn y Cajal in the 19th century. Diagram B shows how dendrites from one neuron receive inputs (i.e, axons) from another neuron.

1. **Motor neurons** convey motor information.
2. **Sensory neurons** convey sensory information.
3. **Interneurons** modulate the activity of other neurons.

All neurons have a basic structure that consists of a **cell body** or **soma**, **dendrites**, and an **axon** (Figure 1.2). The soma contains the genetic material (i.e., DNA) within the nucleus. Neurons develop from stem cells and cannot divide, but the genetic material is needed to produce the proteins required to maintain and regulate neuronal function. Dendrites receive information from other neurons, which is called **electrochemical signaling;**

some have specialized endings that receive information directly from the environment. For example, if you accidentally place your hand on a hot stove, sensory neurons that **innervate** your skin register the potentially damaging heat and activate motor neurons to cause you to withdraw your hand.

Functional magnetic resonance imaging is routinely used to observe nervous system activity in subjects who are performing specific tasks, such as reading or listening to music. Using this technique, one can actually see different regions of the brain processing information. An obvious question to ask is, "What are neurons doing when they are active?" and, more specifically, "If neurotransmission is the universal language of neurons, what is being transmitted by neuronal activity?"

Using the example we presented above of accidentally placing your hand on a hot stove, we can describe what happens on a neuronal level: Heat from the stove activates specific receptors in your skin, which are located in the specialized endings of sensory neuron dendrites. In their resting state (i.e., in the absence of a stimulus that causes them to become active), neurons have an electrical potential across their cell membranes that is derived by preventing sodium ($Na+$) and potassium ($K+$) ions from passively moving between the inside and outside of the cell. Specifically, the neuron works to establish a gradient of $Na+$ and $K+$ ions between the inside and outside of the cell—low $Na+$ inside the cell versus outside the cell and high $K+$ inside the cell versus outside the cell. This ionic gradient, called **membrane potential**, establishes an electrical charge between the inside and outside of the neuron. When the receptors in your skin become activated by the high temperature of the stove, a change in the membrane potential of the sensory neurons is signaled as $Na+$ floods into the cell and $K+$ floods back out of the cell in an attempt to restore the ionic gradient. The flow of ions across the neuronal membrane produces a change in membrane potential called **depolarization.** When it is strong enough, depolarization of the dendrite produces a wave of electrical current that passes into the cell body where an **action potential** is initiated and sent along the neuron's axon. Once the action potential reaches the axon terminal, chemical signals called **neurotransmitters** are released into the space between the axon terminal and the dendrites of the neighboring neuron. This space is called a **synapse**. The release of a neurotransmitter from the axon terminal into the synapse triggers receptors on the neighboring neuron's dendrites that are specific to that neurotransmitter, which, in turn, produces depolarization of the neighboring neuron's dendrites. The neurons that supply the axon and dendrite partners are referred to as the presynaptic neuron and the postsynaptic neuron, respectively. Sufficient stimulation (i.e., postsynaptic depolarization) leads to a new action potential in the postsynaptic neuron.

In our example of a hand getting too close to a hot surface, sensory neurons that are activated by heat synapse onto interneurons in your spinal cord that make direct connections or synapses onto the motor neurons that activate the appropriate muscles to retract the hand. This simple neuronal circuit (sensory neuron to interneuron to motor neuron to muscle) is called a withdrawal reflex as it does not require any conscious activity from your brain to make the limb retract. Such a simple neuronal circuit is missing much of the synaptic complexity that neurons in the brain must deal with in regulating brain function (CNS neurons may make anywhere from 5,000 to 200,000 synaptic connections, depending on the type of neuron—meaning that the average human brain has roughly 100 trillion synapses!). However, this simple reflex illustrates the electrochemical impulse that all neurons use to receive, process, and propagate information throughout the nervous system.

■ **Learn more about neurons and neuronal function** Search the Internet for *neuron and anatomy,* or *neuron and function.*

2 Learning and Memory: A Historical Perspective

OVERVIEW

The human search for knowledge has walked hand-in-hand with the rise of civilization. Throughout history, humans have demonstrated a fascination with the mind and its function in **memory** (the process of retaining and recalling facts, images, and past experience) and **learning** (the process of acquiring skill or knowledge). **Neuroscience**, the study of the structure and function of the **nervous system** as it relates to behavior and learning, is a relatively young discipline. Long before this branch of science emerged, however, laypeople and scholars from all walks of life have shared an interest in the function of the brain. Anyone who stops and considers just how essential the ability to learn and remember is to the human experience cannot help but be amazed by this incredible organ.

In this chapter, we review the history of the study of learning and memory and look at some of the specific contributions made by a few key figures. Elsewhere in this book, we explore the various learning and memory systems in the brain and look at how neurons are organized into neural circuits to produce functionally distinct systems. We also explore the cellular and molecular changes that underlie learning and memory in both animals and humans. Learning appears to result from experience-dependent changes in the way neurons connect in the brain. It is easy to take for granted our capacity for learning and memory, yet medicine and science continually reveal that the brain is a fragile organ, susceptible to stress, disease, and aging. Thus, in the final chapter, we examine the latest efforts to design new medications to enhance or disrupt learning and memory.

Over the years, scientists have learned a great deal about the workings of the brain. The contribution of molecules, the function of neurons and their networks, and the roles played by different regions of the brain in learning and memory have all been worked out to some degree. This knowledge was achieved through the contributions of researchers from many different scientific disciplines. It would be impossible to cover in this book all the individuals and accomplishments that have culminated in our current understanding of learning and memory. Indeed, the neuroscience of learning and memory has been a winding road to travel, with every grain of truth discovered along the way complicated by other facets of the human condition—including religion, politics, and ego. One of the greatest accomplishments in the search to unlock the mysteries of the mind and the function of the brain was the acceptance of the idea that lofty subjects such as learning and memory could even be studied using scientific methods.

COGNITIVISM VERSUS BEHAVIORISM IN THE STUDY OF LEARNING AND MEMORY

The study of learning and memory is, in fact, a quest to understand the relationship of mind and body—a quest that has deep roots in both philosophy and biology. Learning and memory research has roots in a variety of different philosophies and methodological traditions. **Cognitivism** and **behaviorism** are two philosophies that are radically different and have followed repetitive cycles of favor and disfavor among researchers attempting to study learning and memory. Cognitivism focuses on the complex mental components underlying the structure, acquisition, and uses of knowledge—ideas, thoughts, love, feelings, and conscious awareness are just a few examples of the cognitive attributes that are considered from this philosophical perspective. In contrast, behaviorism favors measurable and observable attributes in the study of learning and memory. Mechanistic explanations from a biological perspective are used to explain how an organism reacts or adapts to its environment through genetics and experience.

In addition to the different perspectives inherent to behaviorism and cognitivism, further distinctions are often drawn between the researchers who study learning and memory in humans versus animals. Researchers who study human learning and memory tend to adopt cognitivism, whereas researchers who study learning and memory in animals have traditionally adopted behaviorism. Debates are ongoing over which perspective is the most valuable for understanding learning and memory. Both behaviorist and cognitivist approaches have led to crucial insights in the attempt to understand learning and memory. The same can be said for researchers who study learning and memory in animals and those who study humans. The best research model depends on the specific question being addressed. For example, a cognitivist approach in studies using a rodent yields little information because the complex mental components of learning and memory cannot easily be assessed in animals. You cannot easily ask a rodent how it really felt about having to run mazes to get a cheese reward. In contrast, rodents can be experimentally manipulated to test various aspects of learning and memory that would be unacceptable to test in humans. The behaviorist doesn't really care how the rodent felt about running the maze, nor what its conscious motivation was for failing to do the task, but rather, wants to know if it can still accomplish the task if a specific part of its brain has been removed or damaged.

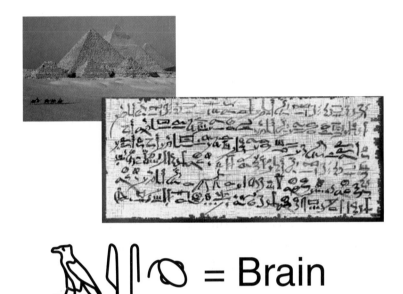

Figure 2.1 The Edwin Smith Surgical Papyrus is the oldest known document describing specific surgical techniques and outcomes. This figure shows portions of the papyrus and the Egyptian symbol for the word *brain*.

THE ORIGIN OF THE STUDY OF LEARNING AND MEMORY

The study of learning and memory traces its beginnings to ancient Egypt. The first written account of the word *brain* and its basic anatomy are recorded in an ancient Egyptian writing around 1700 B.C., termed the Edwin Smith Surgical Papyrus (Figure 2.1). This papyrus is a collection of 48 medical cases, 27 of which are dedicated to head trauma. The writing is presumed to be a compilation of medical practices that date as far back as 3000 B.C. For each medical case, the papyrus annotates the problem, such as "gaping hole in head," then describes the patient's symptoms and whether medical intervention could be employed. The papyrus contains anatomical descriptions for the cerebrospinal fluid (the nutrient-rich fluid that surrounds and cushions the brain and spinal cord), the **meninges** (the outer covering of the brain), as well as the first neurological diagnosis of brain damage resulting in a loss of speech (i.e., aphasia). The author of this papyrus may have been the Egyptian physician Imhotep, regarded by many scholars as the founder of Egyptian medicine and the first true medical doctor. The rational and empirical observations made by Egyptian physicians concerning brain injury do not appear to have crossed into the mysticism and religious beliefs of the priests, as the heart was accorded more importance than the brain. In fact, during the embalming process for mummification, the heart was carefully removed, along with the lung, liver, and stomach, while the brain was simply pulverized in the skull and removed through the nostrils as waste! With the decline of ancient Egypt, medical knowledge about brain function was replaced with speculation and mysticism in many cultures for centuries to come.

Until around 500 B.C., the Greeks and other cultures continued to believe as the Egyptians did—that mental function originated from the heart and that sickness was caused by demons. A Greek physician named Hippocrates (460–380 B.C.) challenged these views with radical arguments concerning both disease and the origin of the mind. Hippocrates rejected the prevailing views that regarded health and illness as functions of superstition or magic, and instead pursued medicine as a branch of science. In his writings, Hippocrates prepared his patients much like the Egyptian physicians did, through careful observation, patient interviews, and detailed recordings of his results. For his contributions to the field, Hippocrates is widely regarded as the father of modern medicine. A student of Hippocrates, Herophilus (335–280 B.C.), practiced dissection on both humans and animals, which allowed him to describe the outer structure of the brain and several other organs. Like Hippocrates, Herophilus recognized that the brain was the organ responsible for intelligence. Herophilus is considered the father of anatomy.

The ancient Greek philosophers Socrates and Plato also considered the topics of learning and memory worthy of contemplation and discussion. In Plato's writings, he likened the mind to a blank slate, like a block of wax to be written on by memories. Plato rejected Egyptian mysticism and championed the idea that the brain, not the heart, was the organ of the mind.

Plato (427–347 B.C.) followed the teachings of Socrates in that he rejected natural philosophy in favor of moral philosophy. In other words, Plato believed that science was an unworthy pursuit because it was acquired through the senses and thus was confused and impure. True knowledge, Plato reasoned, was only gained by a contemplative soul that rejected the world and the senses. Like Hippocrates, Plato believed that the mind was housed in the brain; however, Plato believed that the brain simply housed the intellect or rational part of the soul, which was immortal (see "Plato on Memory" box).

Aristotle (384–322 B.C.) is considered by many scholars to be one of Plato's most gifted students, even though he rejected Plato's moral philosophy in favor of natural science. Aristotle believed that true knowledge could only be obtained from the senses and thus is credited with inventing the **scientific method**, the system of gaining knowledge by raising questions, collecting data through observation and experimentation, formulating hypotheses to answer the original questions, and testing the hypotheses. Aristotle (Figure 2.2) actively searched for connections between learning and memory and between the mind and body in natural science. Aristotle did not consider human dissection acceptable; he therefore elected to perform animal dissections to study the function of the organs in the body. Influenced by Egyptian teachings, he ignored Hippocrates and Plato and concluded that intelligence resided in the heart. Aristotle believed that the brain was an important organ; however, he believed that its purpose was to cool the heart.

Aristotle made a number of important contributions to the study of learning and memory. He noted that memory decreased with old age, and therefore was the first to link memory and **reason** (the ability to think logically). In addition, Aristotle is credited with the first description of the **Law of Contiguity.** This law—which states that when two ideas or events are perceived to have occurred in close association, they are likely to occur again, as the next occurrence of the first idea or event will tend to elicit the other—is the cornerstone of all modern learning theories (see "The Law of Contiguity" box).

Plato on Memory

In the 4th century B.C., Plato wrote, in a dialogue between Socrates and Theaetetus:

> Imagine . . . that our minds contain a block of wax, which in this or that individual may be larger or smaller, and composed of wax that is comparatively pure or muddy, harder in some, softer in others, and sometimes of just the right consistency. . . . Let us call it the gift of the Muses' mother, Memory, and say that whenever we wish to remember something we see or hear or conceive in our own minds, we hold this wax under the perceptions or ideas and imprint them on it as we might stamp the impression of a seal ring. Whatever is so imprinted we remember and know so long as the image remains; whatever is rubbed out or has not succeeded in leaving an impression we have forgotten and do not know.

—Plato, *Theaetetus*

Figure 2.2 Ancient Greek philosopher Aristotle (384–322 B.C.) was the first of the great philosophers/thinkers to link memory and reason.

The Greek physician Galen (A.D. 131–201), like Aristotle, looked for scientific answers for the mind and body debate using dissection and experimentation. Galen did not limit his study to animals because, in his role as physician to the gladiators in Rome, he became adept at human surgery and anatomy. Galen performed experiments on living animals (vivisection) to test his theories, including those related to the function of nerves. Galen championed the idea that **ventricles** (the spaces or cavities within the brain) act as a reservoir for memory. In his model, **spirits**—nonphysical entities that are the substance of all life—flowed into different areas of the ventricles to create memory.

The Law of Contiguity

The Law of Contiguity is a cornerstone of most scientific theories of learning. This law states that after events occur together in space and time, only one of the events is required to evoke a memory of the others. Aristotle believed that knowledge and the mind were constructed from basic sensations, such as desire, pain, pleasure, and the ability to cause motion. He considered visual images to be the subjective side of movement and believed that images anchored to the past represent memories. All animals possessed this memory of the senses; however, voluntary memory distinguished humans from animals. In considering the mechanisms of memory, Aristotle wrote that external movements caused changes in the spirits in the blood, which were linked to the senses. The spirits that Aristotle described were nonphysical entities that flowed through our bloodstream to control behavior. The expression that a person's "spirits are low" comes from this belief and implies that feelings of sadness or melancholy are produced by the depressed nature of the spirit entities.

RATIONALIST AND EMPIRICIST PERSPECTIVES ON LEARNING AND MEMORY

At the turn of the 1st millennium, Greek and Roman scholars undertook studies of the nervous system as the ancient Egyptians had done centuries earlier. Studies of the structure and anatomy of the brain and nervous system progressed steadily up until the 17th century, when a French philosopher and mathematician, René Descartes (1596–1650), radically changed our understanding of brain function and behavior. He provided the first mechanistic account of the relationship of mind and body. Descartes (Figure 2.3), like Plato and many others before him, was a rationalist. The philosophy of **rationalism** states that reason, not the senses, is the only means through which true knowledge can be acquired. In other words, knowledge is not gained through experiences, but through self-evident principles that are implicit in the very notion of reasoning itself. Descartes attempted to reconcile the tension developing between religion and science by proclaiming that the brain and nerves control the actions of the body; however, this control was in direct response to the actions of the animal spirits—forces contained *within* the brain but not *of* the brain. Descartes saw the body as something like a puppet, reflexively acting out the instructions of the nerves and brain under the control of the mind (i.e., the soul). By localizing the soul to the pineal gland, a specific part of the brain, Descartes paved the way for other scientists and philosophers to mechanistically consider the mind and body in terms of the nervous system.

In the Middle Ages, the rationalist view of how knowledge is obtained was challenged by a new philosophy called **empiricism**. Beginning in the 17th century, philosophers such as John Locke (1632–1704), David Hume (1711–1776), and James Mill (1773–1835) proposed that knowledge can be derived only from experience. This belief ran counter to the generally accepted idea that the mind imposes structure on our experiences. The ideology was not all that new, however: Aristotle's teachings made

(A)

Figure 2.3 French philosopher René Descartes **(A)** made this famous drawing of a child's hand over a flame **(B)**. According to Descartes, the fire produces external motions that trigger the peripheral ends of nerve fibrils in the hand. These fibrils extend to the brain, where the mechanical displacement rearranges the flow of the spirits into the appropriate nerves to withdraw the hand.

(B)

Figure 2.3 *(continued)*

clear that he was more of an empiricist than were Plato and most of the rest of his contemporaries, who held views that were more closely aligned with the principles of rationalism.

MULTIPLE MEMORY SYSTEMS: A MODERN VIEW OF LEARNING AND MEMORY

Current theories about learning and memory support a role for multiple systems that can be experimentally dissociated from one another. The birth of this concept is derived from the work of Franz Joseph Gall (1758–1828), a German neuroanatomist and physiologist (Figure 2.4). Known as the father of **phrenology**

Figure 2.4 Gall used the external shape of the skull to determine personality, mental abilities, and moral faculties.

(the study of the structure of the skull as an indicator of a person's mental abilities or character), Gall formulated theories that are considered ludicrous by neuroscientists today; however, there was definitely genius in Gall's theory that mental function was not a unitary event, but rather was localized to different regions of the outer part of the brain, an area called the cerebral cortex. Gall believed that different cerebral cortical areas possessed different aspects of the mind (e.g., mathematics and music), with each zone maintaining specific forms of memory (Figure 2.5). Although Gall's cortical representations were completely wrong, current research has demonstrated that cortical zones do process different forms of sensory information (e.g., auditory and visual information are processed in different regions), suggesting that his concept of multiple memory systems localized in different regions of the cortex was correct. Gall, a

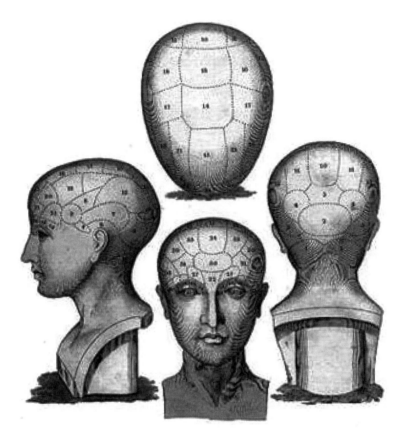

Figure 2.5 Although Gall's map of which areas of the brain controlled various characteristics was wrong, Gall was correct in his belief that different regions did have diverse functions.

competent neuroanatomist, also made important contributions to our understanding of the brain's structure and composition.

The next significant theory regarding the existence of multiple functional systems in the brain was provided by the French philosopher Maine de Biran (1766–1824). Maine de Biran considered memory to have three components: **representative memory**, concerned with recollection of ideas and events; **mechanical memory**, concerned with the formation of skills and habits; and **sensitive memory**, concerned primarily with emotions and feelings.

Although Maine de Biran never attempted to associate his theories with brain anatomy or biology, his theories on the division of specific forms of memory were proven correct, as we discuss in Chapter 4.

American philosopher and psychologist William James (1842–1910) proposed that habits and conscious memory were distinct processes. For example, routine behaviors (e.g., walking, fencing, and singing) were mediated by a series of habits that function on an unconscious level to generate movements and sensations. James viewed the memory of events and facts, however, as a conscious process. He postulated that **recall** (the process of remembering a specific piece of information) was performed using a complex set of associations. A strong memory had a number of strong associations. James was the first to suggest that memory could be separated into short-term and long-term forms. Like Maine de Biran, James never possessed any scientific proof for his theories; however, as we will discuss in Chapters 3 and 4, modern studies of learning and memory support his ideas on a number of levels.

EBBINGHAUS'S NONSENSE

At the turn of the 20th century, the study of the human nervous system was dominated by concepts and beliefs that were largely lacking in scientific proof. In fact, during this period, most scientists considered learning and memory too complex or simply unsuitable for scientific study. German philosopher Hermann Ebbinghaus (1850–1909) became the first person to perform systematic research on verbal learning and memory in humans following a rigorous scientific approach. Ebbinghaus reasoned that the only way to examine pure verbal memory was to create a battery of words of which a test subject would have no prior knowledge or experience. To do this, he created 2,300 nonsense syllables that he produced by randomly inserting a vowel between two consonants (e.g., "RIH" or "GUH"), so that the combination of consonants and vowels did not have any meaning in the English language. By combining these nonsense syllables into series of various lengths, Ebbinghaus described the shape of the first **learning curve**, the mathematical projection reflecting a person's rate of improvement in performing a new task as he or she practices. Ebbinghaus observed that the time required to memorize a nonsense word increased sharply as the number of syllables increased. Ebbinghaus also observed that **retention**, the ability to recall past experience, improved with continual practice. Ebbinghaus discovered that his ability to learn was far better when he practiced the nonsense syllables over several sessions than when he attempted to cram all of the practice into one session (termed *distributed learning* versus *massed learning*). Finally, Ebbinghaus explored the law of association (i.e., contiguity) and found that associations are important and that they occur whether the items are directly next to one another or not. Given the rigor and precision that Ebbinghaus employed in his studies, it should not be surprising that little new information concerning **rote** learning and retention has been added over the last century.

THE NEURON DOCTRINE

The **neuron doctrine** has its roots in the work of Matthias Schleiden (1804–1881) and Theodor Schwann (1810–1882), two German cell biologists. Schleiden's background was in botany, whereas Schwann was a physiologist. Both men asserted that all tissues, including the brain, are made up of cells. The concept that neurons—the cells that carry the signals generated throughout the brain and nervous system—were the functional units of the nervous system blossomed when Italian physiologist Camillo Golgi (1843–1926) developed a staining technique for neurons, which he called the "*reazione nera*" ("black reaction"). The characteristic black outline that formed on the neurons following Golgi's new fixation process led Spanish physician Santiago Ramón y Cajal (1852–1934) to make the most detailed descriptions of neuronal architecture yet recorded. Ramón y Cajal improved on Golgi's staining technique and became convinced that neurons were not physically fused together throughout the nervous system, as Golgi believed. Ramón y Cajal saw individual neurons wherever he looked in the nervous system. In parallel with Ramón y Cajal, Swiss anatomist and physiologist Wilhelm His (1863–1934) identified specific structures of individual neurons, including those that enabled the nerve cells to communicate with one another. In the footsteps of Ramón y Cajal and His, Swiss scientist Auguste-Henri Forel (1848–1931) observed that if the cell body of a neuron died or if an axon was destroyed, degeneration of the cell occurred up to its junction with another cell—further evidence that neurons were not fused. At the beginning of the 20th century, the work of Ramón y Cajal and others clearly demonstrated the following tenets of the neuronal doctrine:

1. Neurons are the functional units of the nervous system.
2. Neurons are not fused together, but rather are distinct, individual cells.
3. Neurons have three main parts: the dendrite, cell body or soma, and axon.
4. Axons terminate and make close connections with the dendrites or somata (plural of *soma*) of other neurons.
5. Neurotransmission—the communication of information through a neuron—is directional in that dendrites pass information to the somata, which then extend into the axon terminals.

SUMMARY

The study of learning and memory has matured over the last 2,000 years. Neuroscience as a discipline developed from philosophy, anatomy, and later, psychology and physiology. In the days of the first Egyptian and Greek physicians, the prevailing view was that the human mind—in this era, "mind" referred not just to the ability to think or reason, but also to the essence of humanity, or "soul"—resided in the heart, not the brain. Learning and memory—if they were considered at all—were regarded as philosophical or spiritual manifestations, not biological processes.

The concept of the brain as the organ of learning and memory began to take root around the turn of the 1st millennium, largely through the observations of physicians such as Hippocrates and Galen. Centuries of research by pioneering anatomists and physiologists supported this view; however, it wasn't until Descartes, in the 17th century, first described a mechanistic explanation for the mind and body relationship that subsequent researchers really began to identify structures of the brain and to explore the relationship between these structures and the processes of learning and memory.

Although neuroscience was increasingly becoming the domain of empirical science and scientists, philosophers continued to make significant contributions to the field. William James's theory regarding the differences between conscious and unconscious memory and Hermann Ebbinghaus's elegant experiments on the effects of practice on learning both provided valuable insight into the ongoing quest to unlock the mysteries of learning and memory. Today, research in learning and memory encompasses numerous scientific disciplines and research paradigms, from basic researchers and medical physicians who study animal models and humans, to psychologists and computer engineers who explore the inner workings of the human mind and silicon technology.

■ **Learn more about the history of neuroscience** Search the Internet for *history* and *neuroscience.*

3 | Forms of Learning

LEARNING DEFINED

If you ask a philosopher, a psychologist, and a neurobiologist to define "learning," you are likely to get three very different answers. You may even get different answers if you ask researchers in the same field of study. Because most of what is known about learning is based on observing changes in behavior, the definition of learning can have very different meanings, depending on the behavior being studied. For example, some definitions state that learning does not occur instantaneously. Some theories define learning as a long lasting change to distinguish it from immediate, automatic responses to **sensory stimuli**. Other definitions restrict learning to only those types of behaviors that are ecologically relevant for an organism's survival. For our purposes, we will consider the broadest possible meaning and simply define learning as an experience-dependent change in behavior (see "Reflexes" box).

FORMS OF LEARNING

At its most basic level, learning is a change in an organism's behavior that occurs in response to experience. We use the word *organism* and not *human* (or, for that matter, *nonhuman primate*, *mammal*, or *vertebrate*) because experienced-based behavior changes can be observed in almost all members of the animal kingdom—from certain types of bacteria that move toward or away from a particular chemical (a phenomenon called *chemotaxis*) to the man who picks up the telephone when it rings. That so many different organisms display this quality suggests that learning is a very important biological characteristic.

Learning can be studied at multiple levels in many different organisms. For example, learning can be explored at the molecular or cellular levels. In addition to humans, worms, flies, and rodents are commonly used to study learning. Researchers exploit the similar behaviors exhibited by these organisms. In this chapter, we examine three forms of learning—**nonassociative learning**, **associative learning**, and **incidental learning**—and the behavioral paradigms that are commonly used to explore them.

Nonassociative Learning

Nonassociative learning may be the most basic form of learning. It has been observed in most of the **eukaryotes** studied to date. Nonassociative learning has two components: **habituation** and **sensitization**.

Reflexes

Immediate responses to sensory stimuli include reflex circuits. For example, when your hand encounters pain (e.g., fire, electricity, or a sharp object), it is immediately retracted away from the harmful environment. Some definitions of learning exclude this behavioral response because it is an innate behavior, a genetically preprogrammed response that is not voluntarily controlled. This protective mechanism is due to the senses forming autonomic (automatic) sensory-motor circuits with the muscle, ensuring a rapid response that is independent of the brain. Other definitions maintain that if the reflex can be modified in an experience-dependent manner, it reflects learning.

Habituation is a gradual reduction in a behavioral response that occurs with repeated presentation of the same (or similar) stimulus. By definition, a habituated response is defined by a loss in an existing response and excludes the effects of fatigue, injury, or drugs. Habituation can be commonly observed all around you. In fact, one reason why you do not respond to many stimuli throughout the day is that you are habituated to them. To illustrate habituation, try this: The next time you catch your cat napping, clap your hands. It is likely that your pet will raise its head and possibly even rise to investigate the noise. If you continue to clap every time your cat takes a nap, however, you will eventually notice that your pet no longer responds and may sleep right through the disturbance.

In the laboratory, habituation is commonly studied in simple organisms, such as the marine mollusk *Aplysia* or the marine worm *Nereis pelagica*. When touched, *Aplysia* withdraws its siphon, or tail. *Nereis,* which lives in the seabed, withdraws readily to the protection of its lair in response to vibration or visual stimuli. Both of these behaviors can be readily habituated with repeated presentation of the appropriate stimulus. Rodents are also easily habituated with relevant biological stimuli. Rats have an acute sense of smell and new smells initiate a change in their sniff frequency. Rats have been observed to increase their breathing rates (a measure of sniffing) from once per second to 8–10 times per second when presented with a new odor. If the smell is repeatedly presented, the rat's **olfactory** (smell-based) response becomes habituated. Importantly, presentation of a new odor produces an increase in breathing rate. This experiment illustrates that a behaviorally relevant response (rats rely on smell as a primary way to interact with their environment) is stimulus specific. Habituated responses do not readily transfer across stimuli.

These examples focus on lower organisms. Do humans habituate to repetitive stimuli? Yes. Parents often observe that newborn babies devote far more attention to a new stimulus than to familiar ones (this has been verified in experiments). The Austrian composer Joseph Haydn—known as the father of the symphony—used repetitive components in his opening theme in Symphony No. 94 in G major *"Surprise"* to lull the audience, who found themselves startled out of their seats during the **dishabituating** full orchestra fortissimo, featuring kettledrums, which Haydn included in the second movement (see "Music and Human Performance" box).

Sensitization is the process of becoming highly sensitive to specific stimuli. Where learning is concerned, the stimuli are generally events or situations. Like habituation, the sensitization response is widespread throughout the animal kingdom. The sensitizing stimulus, unlike the stimuli that produce habituation, is usually strong or noxious. Another important difference is that sensitizing stimuli usually produces an increase in the response to a wide variety of stimuli. Sensitization can be viewed as a priming mechanism, increasing arousal and attention, and lowering the threshold for defensive responses. For example, a leaf falling on a worm that has recently escaped a pecking bird produces a much greater escape response than if the worm had encountered the leaf in the absence of any previous physical assault. Presumably, sensitizing stimuli that generate an enhanced defensive threshold—in this case, an enhanced wiggle response by the worm, immediately following a pecking bird—can be viewed as a beneficial behavior, since the bird may have returned for a second try at its meal.

Associative Learning

Associative learning is a more complex process than nonassociative learning in that it requires two stimuli to be presented closely in time. Both habituation and sensitization are learned nonassociative responses that lack stimulus specificity. After the earthworm is pecked by the bird, it wiggles vigorously when any subsequent physical contact is made, whether it is another attack by the bird or a falling leaf. Unlike nonassociative learning, associative learning involves discrimination between different stimuli. This discrimination permits an organism to draw causal relationships from its environment. For example, a bee sampling nectar in a diverse field of flowers can, upon discovering

Music and Human Performance

Haydn knew that the kettledrum in his Symphony No. 94 in G major "Surprise" would have a startling effect even before his first performance—he was even quoted as saying, "there the ladies will jump." Haydn, along with other composers (e.g., Bach, Beethoven, and Mozart), routinely used powerful dynamic contrasts in their music for emotional effect. The emotional impact induced by the sudden fortissimo chords may elicit the startle reflex, which is associated with specific physiological changes, including changes in posture (arms and legs brought in to the chest), eye blinks, increased heart rate, heightened electrodermal responses, and possibly weeping. Music can indeed be emotionally powerful, but can it affect your ability to learn? Startling music may, at first, seem to decrease cognitive performance because of the physiological responses described above; however, the startle reflex may also elicit arousal (heightened attention), which has been shown to increase long-term memory. Thus, a sudden shock to the ears may actually help you cram for tests! Does low, repetitive background music lull the student to sleep and decrease learning? Opinion is currently divided about this, as both increases and decreases in cognitive test performance have been observed with low-level background music. Thus, using background music while studying may be helpful to some and deleterious to others.

that a particular flower possesses a strong yield of nectar, use information like the location of the field and the color, shape, or pattern of this specific flower to restrict its sampling—greatly enhancing its survival. It is important, however, to consider the adaptability (or **plasticity**) of this response: Because the flower has a high yield of nectar one day does not ensure that this will be the case the next day or the next week. Therefore, the association must be plastic, or modifiable. In the case of the bee, once it begins to find that the yield of nectar in a particular flower is unacceptable, it needs to modify its behavior by sampling other flowers or moving to another field. A failure to make this adjustment will threaten the bee's survival.

The two main categories of associative learning are **classical conditioning** and **instrumental (operant) conditioning**. Classical conditioning, also termed *Pavlovian conditioning*, is named after the Russian physiologist Ivan Pavlov (1849–1936), who performed studies with dogs and is credited with the first experimental descriptions of this form of associative learning (Figure 3.1).

Classical Conditioning

In classical conditioning, a subject is presented with a stimulus that will cause a specific behavioral response. In Pavlov's research, the stimulus was food and the response was salivation. More specifically, the food was the **unconditioned stimulus** (a stimulus that produces an automatic, unlearned response) and the salivation was the **unconditioned response** (a response that is unlearned and automatic). In classical conditioning, the association is produced by pairing a neutral **conditioned stimulus** (a stimulus that initially produces no observable change in behavior) with the unconditioned stimulus. The unconditioned stimulus is typically a biologically relevant stimulus, whereas the experimenter selects the conditioned stimulus based on the qualities or abilities of the test subject. For example, a good conditioned stimulus for a study using dogs would take advantage of

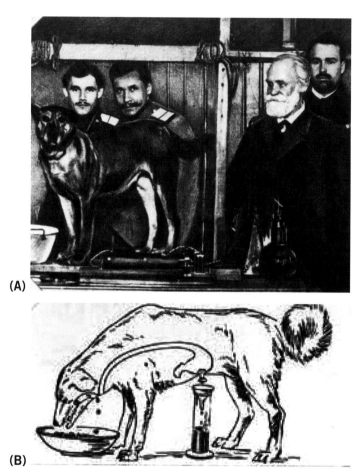

Figure 3.1 Classical conditioning (also known as Pavlovian conditioning) occurs when a natural reflex, such as salivation, becomes associated with a stimulus, such as a whistle or a bell. **(A)** Pavlov (bearded man on right) and his colleagues discovered that the salivary (mouth) and gastric (stomach) secretions that normally occur in dogs at the sight and smell of food could be modified with training. **(B)** After minor surgery, Pavlov was able to collect the salivary and gastric secretions from dogs so that he could learn how sight, hearing, and smell could be used to modify a reflex, such as salivation.

the dog's excellent senses of smell, sight, or hearing. Pavlov used auditory stimuli (bells, metronomes, and whistles) as the conditioned stimulus for his experiments. By presenting the conditioned stimulus and the unconditioned stimulus within a short span of time, Pavlov produced a **conditioned response**, a learned response that is produced by a conditioned stimulus—in this case, a new association between the ringing of a bell and the presentation of food. Pavlov found that the stimulus is specific. In Pavlov's experiments, the tone of the bell was important. Simply generating another auditory stimulus (for example, a whistle) did not produce the unconditioned response.

Using the bee from our example above, a loss of association between nectar and a particular flower (i.e., the bee discovering over time that the flower does not yield sufficient pollen) would lead the bee to modify its learned response (i.e., sample other flowers or move to another field). The loss of a learned behavior is called **extinction** and was demonstrated in Pavlov's experiments. When the conditioned stimulus (i.e., the bell) is applied repeatedly and the unconditioned stimulus (i.e., the food) withheld for multiple presentations, the conditioned stimulus returns to being a neutral stimulus to the subject, as it is no longer associated with anything meaningful.

Instrumental (Operant) Conditioning

Another form of associative conditioning is *instrumental* (or operant) *conditioning*—a term coined by American psychologist Edward Thorndike (1874–1949). It involves the alteration of spontaneous behavioral responses by a reinforcing stimulus.

Using special puzzle-boxes of his own design and construction, Thorndike performed experiments in which the subject (a hungry cat) was conditioned to perform simple tasks (i.e., use a device such as a pulley, lever, or latch to open the puzzle-box door) to obtain food that was in sight but out of reach.

In Thorndike's experiments, the cat was hungry and wanted the food, so it eagerly explored its box. When the cat accidentally tripped the door mechanism, it received its food reward. Thorndike did not believe that the cat understood how the door mechanism worked, but simply increased the frequency of

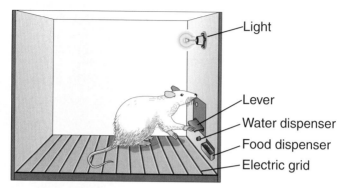

Figure 3.2 Skinner improved on Thorndike's trial and error learning paradigm by building a better box. The Skinner box is a famous research tool in which a test subject presses a lever to obtain a reward, a process called "operant conditioning."

whatever behavior it happened to be doing when the food appeared. Thus, the food served as a reward to reinforce a spontaneous behavior. The term *instrumental* is used to denote the fact that the animal's behavior is essential in producing its reward. Instrumental conditioning is a more complex form of learning than classical conditioning, because the subject must determine which of its actions are responsible for the occurrence of the reinforcer. Remember that in classical conditioning, the subject simply associates whatever specific external event the researcher chooses to pair with the reinforcer.

American psychologist B. F. Skinner (1904–1990) followed Thorndike's lead, designing the **Skinner box** and conducting experiments in operant (instrumental) conditioning (Figure 3.2). In one of Skinner's more unusual learning paradigms, he examined the development of superstitious behavior in pigeons. Skinner placed an automatic food dispenser in a birdcage that would distribute food at regular intervals. The key to this paradigm is that the machine did not attempt to reward a particular behavior, but rather dropped the food into the cage at regular intervals, regardless of the pigeon's behavior. Skinner observed that the pigeon increased the frequency of whatever action it happened to be doing when the food was presented. For example, one bird walked in counterclockwise circles between reinforcements, whereas another pecked in a particular spot in the cage. Skinner had inadvertently revealed superstitious behavior in pigeons by simply reinforcing spontaneous behavior.

Skinner had little doubt that his studies in animals also applied to human behavior, even concerning superstitious behavior. The pigeons' bizarre rituals are similar to the behaviors of humans who come to adopt random behaviors on the belief that they are predictive of a specific outcome. For example, some bowlers believe that bizarre body movements and hand gestures cause their ball to produce a strike. Skinner would argue that the bowler's random movements (either before or after he or she picks up the ball) are reinforced each time a strike is thrown.

In addition to operant conditioning, Skinner also evaluated whether punishment successfully enhanced an animal's ability to learn. Skinner concluded that punishment was not a successful mechanism for altering an animal's behavior. His studies indicated that punishment only taught the subject to avoid the punishment. Following this logic, Skinner argued that prison was not an acceptable solution for criminal activity because the risk of prison for criminal conduct was well established, yet criminal activity did not cease or decline. Skinner maintained that prison only teaches individuals to avoid being imprisoned, not to stop committing crimes.

Incidental Learning

Although both classical and instrumental conditioning are considered forms of complex learning, these paradigms do not exploit the full cognitive potential that many organisms are capable of displaying. Incidental learning, a form of passive learning, is another example of complex learning that can be seen in higher mammals (especially primates) that utilize complex internal representations, such as insight and perception. Learning paradigms that tap into these complex internal representations include maze learning and delayed responses. Using rodents and their innate sensory-motor capacity to navigate mazes, American psychologist Willard Small (1870–1943) observed that rats could learn complex maze patterns to obtain a food reward. (Horror movie buffs should recognize that the Hollywood movie *Willard* was about a man who controlled the behavior of rodents.) Small's maze paradigms for rodents dominated psychology for generations—the popular expression "like a rat in a maze" was coined from Small's experiments. Maze paradigms have evolved over the decades and are still used as behavioral tasks in neuroscience to test complex forms of learning. The Morris Water Maze is one such paradigm that is highly sensitive to spatial learning and the formation of cognitive maps in the hippocampus (discussed in detail in Chapter 6).

Complex learning can also be evaluated using delayed responses. This paradigm requires that the test subject respond to a sensory stimulus (usually visual or auditory) after the stimulus is removed. This method is similar to that used by Ebbinghaus to investigate human visual recognition, except that in delayed response experiments, the time interval before the subject is allowed to respond is extended. In primates, for example, a food treat can be placed in one of two cups that the subject can see. As the subject watches, the contents of the cups are hidden. A blind is then placed between the subject and the two cups with hidden contents. After a set time interval, the blind is removed and the researcher observes how often the subject selects the cup that contains the hidden treat. No learning is assumed to have occurred if the subject selects the correct cup 50% of the time or less (this number represents the number of correct responses that an experimenter would predict if the test subject were simply guessing between two choices). In a modified version of this procedure, called a **delayed nonmatching-to-sample** task, the sub-ject is shown an object and then, after a delay, the object would be paired with a new object, as above. However, using the non-matching-to-sample assay, the researcher would reward the test subject with a treat, such as a squirt of orange juice, only if the new object is chosen. **Delayed matching-to-sample** and delayed nonmatching-to-sample tasks have been highly successful in studying working memory and visual recognition in primates.

■ **Learn more about forms of learning** Search the Internet for *nonassociative learning*, *associative learning*, or *incidental learning*.

4 Stages of Memory and the Brain's Memory Systems

MEMORY DEFINED

If learning is defined as an experience-dependent change in behavior, then memory is the persistence of this behavior change over time. Learning is what makes an organism adaptable, and humans possess a remarkable capacity to translate experience into behavioral changes. Memory, however, is what permits the behavioral change to endure. If our seemingly unlimited capacity to learn is part of what separates humans from the other animals, it is memory that makes learning unlimited in scope and time.

Memory can seem unpredictable at times. A long-forgotten address or phone number can surface at an unexpected time. Sights, smells, or sounds can trigger a distant memory. Your experiences from today alone—the conversations you had, the places you visited, the smells or sounds you noticed when you entered the cafeteria—will shape the person you will be tomorrow, thanks to your ability to learn and remember.

In our simple definitions of learning and memory, we neglected to consider the fact that most of the information and stimuli that we process is *not* destined for memory. Moreover, our definition does not address the fact that memories can be forgotten. For example, on your ride or walk to school this morning, you processed a huge amount of information that you could not recall by the time you got to school: What kind

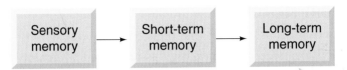

Figure 4.1 The flow of memory appears to be linear. Sensory memory and short-term memory are in close proximity to learning, whereas long-term memory reflects learning in the distant past (months or years ago).

of jacket was the person sitting behind you on the bus wearing? How many cars drove through the intersection while you waited for the "walk" signal to flash? Information that you processed while boarding the school bus or obeying traffic signals was quickly replaced by new information as you arrived at school and walked to your locker. As your inability to recall the phone number of your local pizza delivery place—or what shirt you wore two days ago—demonstrates, the majority of the information you process day in and day out is not destined for memory.

Although it is not yet known why some memories last a lifetime and others are quickly forgotten, advances have been made into understanding the process of memory formation. In this chapter, we illustrate that memory is a process best described by multiple systems rather than one simple mechanism. In examining the three basic stages of memory—sensory (or immediate), short-term (or working), and long-term—we see that the flow of memory can be divided into a series of time-based stages (Figure 4.1). As memory flows through these stages, the sensory inputs (i.e., environmental information) are filtered so that fewer pieces of information end up in **long-term memory** than in either sensory or **short-term memories**. In addition, we examine the different forms of long-term memory and discuss the controversy surrounding "photographic memory."

SENSORY MEMORY

Every sensation or stimulus that registers with your senses—taste, touch, vision, smell, and hearing—is registered by **sensory memory**. A subtype of sensory memory can be defined for each sensory modality. **Iconic memory** (visual stimuli) is commonly studied in humans and other primates, although **haptic memory** (touch) and **echoic memory** (hearing) are also evaluated. Sensory memory—sometimes referred to as **immediate memory**—appears to act as a gateway into the short- and long-term stages of memory.

Sensory memory can be readily studied by limiting the exposure time of a stimulus—for example, by asking test subjects to recount letters flashed on a screen for only a fraction of a second. In this iconic memory test, you would have little trouble responding with the correct answer if you were permitted to answer immediately (i.e., within 1 to 2 seconds) after the presentation of the visual stimulus. If you were asked after more time had passed, you would find it difficult to recall the letter that was flashed on the screen. Sensory memories are extremely short-lived (typically between one-fifth of a second and a few seconds). Most stimuli that trigger sensory memory are lost before they reach short- or long-term memory. The advantage of having a brief sensory memory is that it produces a filter, or buffer, against the vast amount of unimportant stimuli that bombard your senses. This spares your short- and long-term memory from being filled with trivial details—for example, the colors of each passing car on the highway or the hardness of every chocolate chip in a cookie. Should your attention become focused on a particular stimulus, perhaps because it is unusual or has emotional significance, sensory memory will pass it along to the short-term memory.

SHORT-TERM MEMORY

which is also known as **working memory**, resides between your sensory memory and long-term memory. Think of the short-term memory as the scratch pad for sensory memory—providing a temporary place for sensory memory to put information that may or may not be important down the road. Short-term memory is a great asset to sensory memory. For example, if you only had the capacity to store information for a very short time (milliseconds to seconds), you would have a very difficult time making sense of long sentences, such as the one you are now reading, which is certainly very long, indeed! Without short-term memory, you would have forgotten the beginning of the sentence by the time you reached the end. If you had no short-term memory, your mind would simply deal with stimuli in real time, and thus be incapable of determining the context (or "bigger picture") encoded within all of the bits of a stimulus. Because of your short-term memory, you will likely remember the context of a sentence as you read it, even if you do not remember *exactly* how it was worded. This illustrates that short-term memory, like sensory memory, is also limited in time and capacity (see "Action Item: Urgent!" box).

Short-term memory can be easily evaluated using a recall test, in which a subject is asked to recall letters or words from a list. Consistent with Ebbinghaus's observations (see Chapter 1), rehearsing (i.e., repeating the items over and over mentally, verbally, or in writing) is a common way to assist short-term memory and is often associated with transitioning a short-term memory into a long-term memory (as in studying for a test). To assess pure short-term memory, a researcher must prevent the

Action Item: Urgent!

Do you ever feel a sense of urgency to complete a task as soon as it occurs to you? The desire you feel to complete a task when it surfaces in your memory is actually your mind's way of attempting to accomplish the task before you forget about it.

test subject from attempting to preserve or extend the memory. Rehearsal is typically prevented by occupying the subject with a second task during the recall analysis. For example, the experimenter may ask a subject to count back from 100 by threes immediately after being shown the recall list. The generation of this numerical sequence ("100 . . . 97 . . . 94 . . . etc.") prevents the subject from rehearsing the list, thus providing the researcher with a clear glimpse into pure short-term memory.

Short-term memory has been shown to have a capacity of between five and nine items. This was first determined by Princeton University psychology professor George A. Miller, whose defining work, "The Magical Number Seven, Plus or Minus Two: Some Limits on Our Capacity for Processing Information," was based on a series of short-term memory tests that examined the number of items that can be remembered by an individual after a single exposure (see "The Magic of the Seven-Digit Phone Number" box). Interestingly, echoic memories (sounds) can be held longer than iconic memories (visual information). Thus, the number of items that can be held in short-term memory (though always between five and nine items) is influenced by the sense being tested. Short-term memory, like sensory memory, is limited in both capacity and time. Rather than decaying in milliseconds to seconds, however, short-term memory can last up to 20 seconds. Both sensory memory and short-term memory are limited in capacity and time. This suggests that the majority of information that your brain processed is not going to be subject to recall. Can you think of everyday examples where it is more important to remember some things than others? For example, do you think it is more important that you remember the color of every passing car or that a red light means stop?

LONG-TERM MEMORY

Unlike sensory and short-term memories, —as the name implies—is able to retain information over extended periods of time. "Extended," in this case, means minutes, hours, or a life-time. Long-term memory can transfer information out of short-term (working) memory into a more stable medium that is less sensitive to interference or disturbance (i.e., from incoming sensory information).

The Magic of the Seven-Digit Phone Number

Given that short-term memory is best suited to hold seven items, it is beneficial that phone numbers are typically seven digits. Do you find yourself repeating phone numbers over and over as you prepare to make a phone call? Just as rehearsal can be used to extend the longevity of short-term memory, mnemonics—the development of mental strategies to retain information—are often used to assist memory. One example of a mnemonic is to take advantage of the brain's ability to learn words better than a series of random numbers. The next time you want to remember a phone number, instead of rehearsing the number (or writing it down), see if you can construct a word or saying based on the alpha-numeric representations of the number as found on the phone's keypad. A word or phrase takes advantage of your brain's ability to chunk individual pieces of information into larger sets of information. "Chunking" was described by Princeton University psychology professor George A. Miller as a mechanism to extend or assist short-term memory. If you see a string of 15 random letters (I-A-C-D-C-B-O-O-K-I-B-M-F-B-I), the 7 +/− 2 letters you can store dictates that you would not have much luck in recalling this string of letters in a short-term memory test. If you looked for words or acronyms you are familiar with (e.g., ACDC, BOOK, IBM, or FBI), however, you may be able to group (or chunk) the parts of the string in a way that makes it easier for your short-term memory to retain.

Long-term memory can be experimentally separated into two main categories: **declarative memory** and **procedural memory**. Declarative memory (also known as **explicit memory**) stores factual information; procedural memory (also known as **implicit memory**) stores knowledge relating to skills and is difficult to express verbally. Knowing your phone number, locker combination, or the capital of Alaska are all examples of declarative memory. Some examples of procedural memory include riding a bike, serving a tennis ball, and reading. Thus, declarative memories are often characterized as textbook facts—answers to "what" and "who"-type questions—whereas procedural memories are often regarded as "know-how"—the ability to perform a task without having any conscious knowledge of how you do it.

DECLARATIVE (EXPLICIT) MEMORY

Declarative memory is based on pairing a specific stimulus with a fact. For example, if you are asked, "Who was the first president of the United States of America?", you are asking your brain to produce a defined answer based on a previously established association. In this example, you can only know the correct answer if you had previously encountered somewhere in your education the fact that George Washington was the first president of the United States. The act of accessing declarative memory is a deliberate, conscious one—usually in an effort to describe something (**semantic memory**) or recall an event that occurred in the past (**episodic memory**). Semantic memory can be illustrated by letters, words, symbols, or numbers, and represents a person's overall knowledge of the world. If you are a good Trivial Pursuit® player, you have excellent semantic memory. One important difference between semantic memory and episodic memory is in their relationship with time. Knowledge stored in semantic memory is time-independent. For example, remembering when you learned your multiplication tables is not necessary to knowing that 25 is the answer to 5 × 5. Episodic memory, however, requires remembering where and when you acquired the information. For example, if a song reminds you of a particular place or experience in your life, or if the smell of burning hair reminds you of a bad experience you once had in chemistry lab, you are using your episodic memory. Episodic memory is unique to each person, as it reflects the faces, places, smells, sounds, and facts that represent that person's life experiences. Researchers believe that recalling an episodic memory requires the brain to access multiple memory systems to reconstruct the memory. This suggests that, unlike the memories tied to your semantic memory, which are usually factual in nature and thus highly specific, episodic memories are prone to inaccuracies.

How can a memory be inaccurate when we defined this process as the persistence of a learned response? Researchers define the construction of false memories as **confabulation** or **refabrication**; an attempt by the mind to recombine bits and pieces of truth and reality into a cohesive memory. Confabulation or refabrication occurs when a distant memory of high emotional or personal significance is only partially recalled. The overall picture of the memory is intact, but the details are vague or missing. Through elaboration and embellishment, the mind attempts to replace the information that is unclear or missing with details that *could* or *seem* to be true. Refabricated memories seem like reality to the mind, and eventually, become impossible to separate from complete, actual memories.

PROCEDURAL (IMPLICIT) MEMORY

Procedural memories differ from declarative memories because they are not recalled consciously and are not easily forgotten. When people describe a skill as "just like riding a bike," they are usually referring to the fact that once you learn to perform the task, it will always be available to your memory. Procedural memories are nondeclarative, as they lack the quality of being expressed verbally. Can you describe to someone how to ride a bicycle without actually having the person get on the bike and do it? This morning you brushed your teeth and walked or drove to school without being consciously aware of moving the toothbrush or moving your hands as you steered your car from home to the school parking lot. Thus, procedural memories are often considered automatic—if you can do a procedural memory task, you will find yourself performing the task with little recollection of how you do it. Do you think it would be helpful to tell a child learning to ride a bicycle, "Hold the handle bars, pedal, and stay upright"? Hitting a tennis ball seems mechanical to the beginner. After years of playing, however, the swing, footwork, and racquet preparation necessary to play tennis become unconscious events, which is to say that they have become part of the procedural memory.

Procedural memories are typically motor activities, such as riding a bicycle, swinging a tennis racket, learning to touch-type, or playing a musical instrument or a video game. Procedural memories can be any activity that you have learned through trial and error, including nonmotor activities such as reading and learning a language. Watching a child learn to read can be as frustrating for the teacher as it is for the student. It is so easy and always tempting to simply finish the word or sentence before the novice can slowly and methodically sound out each part of each word. You probably have no memory of your own experiences of learning to read, nor the ability to verbally describe how you do it.

Priming is a process in which exposure to a stimulus makes it easier to recall information related to the stimulus at a later time. Priming is an important subtype of procedural memory. One way to demonstrate priming is for subjects to look at a long list of words, as is done in typical recall experiments. Instead of asking the test subject to recall the words entirely from memory, however, the researcher provides the subject with fragments of the words to assess whether partial information is enough to allow successful recall. That is, the researcher determines whether the subject can remember any words from a long list after being given hints. For example, if *procedural* was included in a long list of words, the subject might be asked whether the abbreviated word *pro———* was on the list. Although the list is far too long for the test subject to recall many of the words, researchers consistently find that subjects who are primed perform better than subjects who must recall the word from memory alone. In other words, the subject does not require conscious recollection of a specific word to have access to it in his or her memory. This priming experiment is important because it suggests that stimuli that are not consciously processed may influence our behavior.

MNEMONIC DEVICES AND PHOTOGRAPHIC MEMORY

Have you ever wished you had a better memory? Most people do. Generally, however, people do have a remarkable ability to compensate for their less-than-perfect memories. For example, a person who has trouble remembering the *exact* number of his or her gym locker can adopt a strategy of using a locker in the same general area of the locker room, then selecting a locker that has an unusual-looking lock. Alternatively, he or she could use a **mnemonic device** as a memory aid. Mnemonic devices are strategies that help our memories store and retrieve information. Simple mnemonic devices include repetitions, rhymes, and imagery. "Thirty days has September. . . ," is a mnemonic device for remembering the number of days in each month. Thus, humans have developed many ways to cope with an imperfect memory.

Imagine what it would be like to possess a memory so clear, reliable, and accurate that it was like a photograph. If you have ever experienced a memory so emotionally charged or important that you can close your eyes and recall it in as much detail and clarity as when you first experienced it, you may have experienced what it is like to possess **eidetic imagery**.

Examples of people with a photographic-like memory are rare. Eidetic imagery is the ability to remember an image in so much detail, clarity, and accuracy that it is as though the image were still being perceived. Eidetic imagery is not perfect, as it is subject to distortions and additions (like episodic memory), and vocalization interferes with the memory. Children possess far more capacity for eidetic imagery than adults, suggesting that a developmental change (such as acquiring language skills) may disrupt the potential for eidetic imagery.

Most scientists attribute extraordinary memory performance to an enhanced ability to associate or organize the information to be memorized, rather than true eidetic memory. For example, many expert chess players possess a remarkable capacity to recall the position of chess pieces at any point from a game. The ability to retain an accurate mental image of the chessboard permits these players to play multiple boards at a time—even while they are blindfolded! It was not surprising, then, when researchers observed that expert chess players have a much greater aptitude to remember chessboard patterns compared to test subjects who do not play chess. However, if researchers challenged the expert chess players with randomly generated board patterns, the expert players were no better than novice chess players at recalling chessboard patterns. Thus, by changing the "rules" of the game, researchers revealed that the remarkable capacity of these players to memorize visual information specific to chess (possibly the very reason these individuals are gifted at chess) was not the equivalent of photographic memory. Individuals with true eidetic memory should, by definition, be able to assimilate and recall with perfect detail even random visual scenes (see "Photographic Memory" box).

FUTURE PERSPECTIVES

Everyday experiences teach us that memory can sometimes be perfect and at other times incomplete and unreliable.

Understanding how memories are formed, retained, and lost is of great interest to physicians and philosophers. Memories are a collection of our experiences and are an essential component of what makes each of us unique. Thus, in a philosophical context, one's individuality is defined by memories.

Photographic Memory

Elizabeth, an artist and teacher at Harvard University, was considered to have true eidetic memory. Elizabeth was a rarity in the world of exceptional memories, because she was an adult and did not appear to use any mnemonic representations. Elizabeth was unlike a young man known as "S," who also possessed what appeared to be a limitless memory. "S," who was studied for 30 years by Russian psychologist A. R. Luria, used visual imagery to map and hold each item to be memorized. "S" could line up the items in imaginary place maps in his mind and then simply walk backward through the list to reconstruct each and every item he had committed to memory. Elizabeth did not appear to use mental strategies to organize her unusual memory. When Elizabeth was tested by Charles F. Stromeyer in 1970, he chose to use stereograms (seemingly random patterns of thousands of dots) to disrupt any potential for Elizabeth to use mnemonic representations to organize her memory. Elizabeth could be presented with a stereogram to one eye and then, from memory, superimpose the first image with a second image shown to the other eye. Elizabeth could take the mental image she had made and overlay it with a new image of dots to perform stereopsis (find depth and images) in her mind as long as it was within 10 seconds of seeing the first image. Astonishingly, instead of visual images fading from her mind, the memory of the image would dim and break up in pieces.

Understanding how memories are formed, stored, and retrieved might permit researchers to design drugs that can influence and improve these processes. Enhancing memory could help you in your final exams, your SAT score, and your grade-point average. Think of the benefits that memory-enhancing therapies could bring to people who have had their memories robbed and lifestyles destroyed by **senility** and **Alzheimer's disease**. Also, there is a great need in psychology to be able to effectively repress some memories. Some people are troubled by traumatic experiences to such an extent that it interferes with their day-to-day lives. For example, many combat soldiers suffer from a condition called **post-traumatic stress disorder**, in which they are haunted by memories of the violent, often profoundly disturbing, events of their service. These memories can cause problems that range from emotional distress to physical debilitation. The potential use of drugs to affect memory is discussed in Chapter 9.

We have all experienced an embarrassing moment when a fact or a name that we know well vanishes into thin air ("It's on the tip of my tongue . . ."), only to surface some time later when we have little use for it. The phenomenon behind this example is the subject of a great debate among scientists who study memory: Are memories truly erased, or are they simply unable to be retrieved? Currently, researchers do not understand how seemingly important pieces of information can be lost while trivial facts can be recalled, or how specific memories can be triggered by small and seemingly insignificant cues. For example, in a decade or so, the memories that surface when you attend your first high school reunion may be triggered by the smell of the old cafeteria, the sight of a close friend you have not seen or talked with in years, or even the sound of a song that you have not heard since prom night. Memory is a complex process involving multiple systems and, as we discuss later in this book, can be compromised by trauma to the brain as well as age.

SUMMARY

The storage and recall of memories occur as the result of several processes. There are three stages of memory that serve key roles in memory formation. Sensory (immediate) memory processes information taken in through the senses and acts as a filter to screen out information that is unimportant. Information that may be of significance is permitted to pass from sensory memory to a temporary storage area called short-term (working) memory. If this information is of importance or interest, it is transferred into long-term memory (in some ways, the brain's "hard drive"), where it has the best chance of being available when needed in the future.

Information stored in long-term memory is divided into two categories: declarative memory for information that is event-based (episodic memory) or specific and factual (semantic memory), and procedural memory for information that relates to the performance of tasks that can be done without conscious effort. Episodic memories cannot always be recalled with complete accuracy, as the details that make them up can be distorted and fabricated through a process termed confabulation or refabrication.

A person's ability to recall information can be aided through the use of certain strategies. These strategies include priming, in which clues related to a stimulus help in the recall of the stimulus, and the use of mnemonic devices, which are tricks or shortcuts devised to make it easier to recall specific pieces of information. Individuals with true eidetic imagery can recall visual information with an incredible degree of accuracy and detail. However, individuals with a photographic-like memory are in fact, quite unusual, as this condition appears to be lost in childhood and is rare in adults.

■ **Learn more about the brain's organization of memory** Search the Internet for *sensory memory*, *short-term memory*, or *long-term memory*.

Memory Organization

SEARCH FOR THE MEMORY ENGRAM

The Roman philosopher and statesman Marcus Tullius Cicero (106–43 B.C.) wrote, "The life given us by nature is short, but the memory of a life well spent is eternal." Our memories begin shortly after our birth and are enriched by life's experiences, always just a thought away. Where and how is learning stored in the living matter that is our brain? The answer to this question is believed to reside in the **memory engram**, the neurobiological foundation of memory—and the holy grail of neuroscience.

The search for the memory engram has been a formidable quest. The first step was to localize learning and memory to the brain. As we discussed in Chapter 2, the idea that the brain is the organ for learning and memory was initially rejected in ancient Egyptian and Greek cultures. Rather, the heart was considered the seat of the mind and behavior, an assertion that was propagated for centuries simply because an animal could not survive if the heart was removed or damaged. In the years from the time of Aristotle (384–322 B.C.) through the Age of Enlightenment (18th century Europe), it came to be recognized that the heart, like the other organs of the body, was essential to the body and the brain, and that the brain was the seat of the mind and behavior. As the Spanish physician Santiago Ramón y Cajal (introduced in Chapter 2) wrote in his memoirs:

To know the brain is equivalent to ascertaining the material course of thought and will, to discovering the intimate history of life in its perpetual duel with external forces; a history summarized, and in a way engraved, in the defensive neuronal coordinations of the reflex, of instinct and of the association of ideas.

In revealing the organization and structure of neurons in the brain, Ramón y Cajal and others focused the search for the memory engram on the brain and the cellular organization of neurons.

A student of the neurosciences might ask, "How does one look for the memory engram experimentally?" In the 1920s, American neurophysiologist Karl Lashley (1890–1958) trained rats in a maze-learning task and then produced **lesions** (localized areas of injury) in specific areas of the rodents' brains (thus inactivating the affected areas) to see if maze performance was localized to specific populations of neurons (Figure 5.1). After 30 years of experiments, Lashley concluded that no single area in the brain appeared to be necessary for long-term memory. Although behavioral deficits proportional to the extent of the lesion (i.e., bigger lesions produced bigger behavioral deficits) were found, this observation was not location specific. Lashley summarized his life's work in a famous 1950 article titled "In Search of the Engram." It was in this article that Lashley concluded that there is no distinct memory storage area in the cerebral cortex and that memory is distributed throughout the brain.

COMPLEX TASKS AND LEARNING AND MEMORY

Lashley's search for the memory engram was rooted in reductionist traditions, as championed by the behaviorist Ebbinghaus. These traditions supported the idea that memory is a unitary event of the brain produced by simple associations. Thus, Lashley assumed that his maze-learning task was a simple leaning and memory event and that the lesions he produced in his

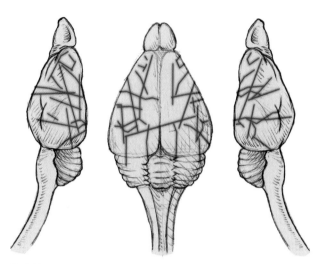

Figure 5.1 Examples of lesions produced in the brains of rodents from Lashley's study of learning and memory. Each red line represents the location of tissue destruction.

subjects' brains would disrupt this process. Lashley's conclusion that learning and memory is not localized to any specific region of the brain fails to consider the possibility that maze learning in rodents is a complex behavioral task that utilizes multiple sensory cues and cognitive functions (i.e., combinations of tactile, olfaction, and visual learning). If Lashley's maze task resulted in recruiting multiple learning and memory systems, then the distributed memory findings that he observed are consistent with the discrete lesions reducing only a part of the learned behavior because other memory systems remained intact.

Lashley's conclusions suggest that the behaviorist tradition has a significant limitation: Animal researchers cannot simply ask the test subject (in this case, a rat) to report what strategies it used to accomplish a complex behavior (in this case, maze learning). Researchers are forced to assume or experimentally define the aspects of learning and memory that are being analyzed. This means that attention to detail is *crucial* when using behavioral animal models to test learning. For example, the Morris Water

Maze, a refined version of maze learning, involves placing a rodent swimming in a large tank of opaque liquid (usually diluted white paint). To stop swimming, the rodent must remember the location of a platform hidden just below the surface. This analysis is believed to rely primarily on spatial learning because visual cues in the room (e.g., pictures and signs) are crucial to direct the rodent where to look for the platform. Experimenters must note even the most trivial details because they have no way of identifying all of the sensory cues the test subject uses to accomplish the task. For example, any of the following details can influence the results: orientation of the maze in the room, lighting, presence of air currents, how the rodent is moved from its cage to the maze, where the researcher stands during the task, and even how the researcher places the rodent into the tank.

In animal model studies, experimenters attempt to isolate the relevant sensory and cognitive functions of learning and memory; however, these studies are limited in that animals may use cognitive functions and sensory cues that the researcher is not aware of. In humans, specific learning and memory systems are easier to study because test subjects can describe the strategies they use. Human behavioral research, however, also has limitations. For example, subjects are often not able to describe their behavioral strategies accurately or may attempt to respond in ways that they believe will be perceived positively by the experimenter. In addition, for ethical reasons, researchers do not produce lesions in the human brain before or after a learning and memory task—making it impossible to duplicate the study design Lashley used with his rodents. Unfortunately, patients with brain damage do exist. Head trauma and neurological diseases that target the nervous system—for example, epilepsy, stroke, and **Korsakoff's syndrome** (memory loss that results from vitamin B deficiency and is commonly seen with severe alcoholism)—can produce brain lesions. Patients with these (and similar) conditions provide a rare opportunity to study the role of the human brain in specific forms of learning and memory. One such patient was a young man known in medical circles as H. M., who—as a result of a treatment undertaken to treat his epilepsy (a brain disorder that produces seizures)—became a very important source of information about brain function and memory.

H. M., AMNESIA, AND SELECTIVE LEARNING AND MEMORY DISORDERS IN HUMANS

After his 16th birthday, H. M. found that the minor seizures he had experienced since the age of 10 were becoming life-threatening. H. M. discovered that his ability to function independently was severely compromised by his epilepsy. Epilepsy is graded based on the severity of the impairment it produces. H. M.'s epilepsy had escalated into a severe form and he was having many seizures every week. The consequences of these episodes—loss of consciousness and severe muscle spasms—prevented H. M. from holding a job, driving a car, or performing any routine activity. Because H. M. did not respond to anticonvulsant medications, his family turned to experimental surgery to stop his seizures. In 1953, when H. M. was 27 years old, he was admitted to Hartford Hospital in Connecticut for radical surgery (Figure 5.2). The surgeon, William Scoville, intended to prevent H. M.'s seizures by performing a bilateral medial temporal lobe resection. Scoville would remove H. M.'s hippocampus and the surrounding cortex in an effort to stop the seizures. Distributed memory systems, as postulated by Lashley, should permit H. M.'s brain to tolerate a relatively small, 8-centimeter (3-inch) brain lesion. Thus, the potential for brain function deficits following the surgery was thought to be a better choice than leaving H. M. with seizures that were growing more frequent and disruptive with every passing year.

H. M. appeared to recover quickly from his surgery. More importantly, the seizures, although not completely eliminated,

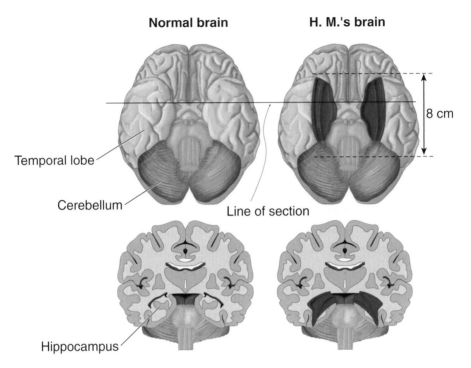

Figure 5.2 This diagram shows H. M.'s brain after surgery in which neurosurgeons attempted to remove the hippocampus and surrounding cortex to cure H. M. of severe epilepsy. The red areas show that both hippocampi have been removed, as well as the surrounding cortical tissue. At left is a diagram of a normal brain for comparison.

were reduced in severity. A full psychological profile revealed that H. M.'s intelligence quotient (IQ) had actually increased after his surgery, primarily due to a higher score in math, and that he possessed normal perception, abstract thinking, reasoning, and motivation. Further psychological evaluation revealed that H. M. had suffered a mild **retrograde amnesia** (a form of memory loss in which a person is unable to remember events that occurred before a brain injury). H. M. had no recollection of having surgery or of the events that occurred immediately before he entered the hospital. Brain surgery (and head trauma in general) is typically accompanied by a loss of memory for events that occurred around the time of the incident, so H. M.'s amnesia did not surprise or trouble the doctors. H. M. retained all of his childhood memories; however, his ability to form new memories was lost. The doctors were puzzled by the fact that, two years after the surgery, H. M. still maintained that the year was 1953—the year of his operation.

H. M. tested well below average in his ability to recall stories or pictures on the **Wechsler Memory Scale**, a test that evaluates learning, memory, and working (short-term) memory. On the word association component of the test, H. M. scored a zero on the difficult words and never showed any improvement, even with repeated practice. Astonishingly, as H. M. cycled through the various tasks of this test, he could not remember the nature of the previous task once he started a new one. If the researchers repeated a task, H. M. could not even recognize that he had already taken the test.

To say that H. M. could not acquire any new memories would be incorrect because, like other people with amnesia, H. M. had an intact procedural memory (see "Procedural Learning Task" box). For example, H. M. had little difficulty learning to read backwards, solving complex puzzles like the Tower of Hanoi puzzle, or **mirror tracing** (drawing backwards—all examples of procedural memory). A person with amnesia, however, never realizes that he or she can perform the task in question. If you ask a person with amnesia about his or her ability to perform a task that normally requires a great deal of practice, the response is usually something like, "I have always been good at puzzles" or "I thought everybody could do this." In terms of the multiple memory system theory we described in Chapter 3, H. M. is considered to have normal procedural memory, but a portion of his declarative memory (episodic and semantic) has been erased. If you ask H. M. his name, birth date, or even the directions to a grade-school friend's house, he has the correct answers because his declarative memory predating the surgery is intact. H. M. will, however, never add to these declarative memory stores. Every person H. M. meets will always be a stranger, no matter how many times he has been introduced to or sat and talked with this person.

Procedural Task Learning

Do you want to learn a procedural task like reading backwards or solving the Tower of Hanoi Puzzle? Start by trying to decipher a few sentences reflected in a mirror. Initially, you will find that recognizing individual words is a daunting task. With practice, however, you will soon be able to read backwards with little effort! With repeated practice, H. M. and other people with global amnesia display steady improvement in the ability to read backwards. The difference, however, is that they simply never consciously know there is improvement, as the task is perceived as being new each time it is attempted. An ancient puzzle like the Tower on Hanoi (or a newer version, the Tower of London) taps into procedural learning skills and also requires substantial practice to accomplish. In its most simple configuration, the Tower of Hanoi is designed from three poles in a line. At the start of the game, three disks of varying diameter must be moved from one pole to another. In this simple example, the Tower of Hanoi solution requires only seven moves to move the objects to another pole with the following rules: Only one disk may be moved at a time and you cannot stack a larger disk on top of a smaller disk. More complex variants of these puzzles have more disks and poles so that hundreds of moves are needed to successfully perform the task. See http://www.lilgames.com/hanoi.shtml to learn more about the Tower of Hanoi Puzzle.

Moving information from short-term to long-term memory is referred to as **consolidation**. The gradients of retrograde amnesia observed in humans with brain damage support the existence of a consolidation phase between short-term and long-term memories. Studies of people with amnesia suggest that consolidation may involve the interaction of multiple brain systems over days to months to years. H. M. possesses normal immediate (sensory) memory and demonstrates the ability to benefit from recent exposures (i.e., priming). In addition, H. M. appears to possess memories predating his surgery, suggesting that his long-term memory is intact. Studies on H. M. and other people with amnesia confirm that short-term and long-term memories are distinct processes—vindicating William James, who theorized that routine behaviors (for example, walking or opening a door) were controlled through unconscious processes, whereas remembering facts and events was a conscious process (see Chapter 2). Thus, H. M. exhibits an extreme case of global amnesia. Although his short-term memory and procedural skills are largely intact, his ability to consolidate declarative memories has been lost.

THE LIMBIC SYSTEM OF THE BRAIN

The neuroanatomy of H. M.'s global amnesia indicates that the area around the medial temporal lobes, including the hippocampus and surrounding cortical areas, are critical for the formation of declarative memories (as well as explicit memories—see Chapter 4). The extent of H. M.'s surgical lesion has been confirmed using magnetic resonance imaging (MRI, a noninvasive scanning procedure of brain activity), demonstrating that Dr. Scoville had indeed removed the hippocampus and surrounding cortex as intended. There have been a number of cases of amnesia with varying degrees of memory dysfunction. For example, patient R. B. developed global amnesia following complications during heart surgery.

During his surgery, R. B. developed cerebral ischemia (a lack of oxygen to the brain) as a result of the loss of blood flow to his brain. R. B. possessed learning and memory deficits similar to H. M.'s, and a post-mortem analysis (R. B. died a few years after his surgery) indicated that R. B.'s brain damage was restricted primarily to the hippocampus. Another patient, N. A., was accidentally stabbed through the nostril with a fencing foil. The blade appeared to have made its way to the base of the brain in the thalamus. Initially, N. A. showed **anterograde amnesia** (loss of memory for events that follow an injury to the brain) and lost about 2 years from retrograde amnesia. Compared to H. M. and R. B., N. A. displayed modest improvement over time and appeared to have more selective dysfunction in verbal memory compared to nonverbal tasks.

The extent of amnesia varies among H. M., R. B., N. A., and other patients with amnesia. All of these individuals suffer from damage to the structures of the brain that are essential to memory, emotion, and consciousness—structures known collectively as the limbic system (Figure 5.3). The limbic system includes the cortex surrounding the temporal lobe and several structures buried beneath the cortex, including the amygdala, hippocampus, and thalamus. The limbic system appears to be the conduit for connecting higher and lower brain function, as it shares connections with virtually all parts of the brain. Damage to structures within the limbic system, including the hippocampus in nonhuman primates, is associated with defective learning and memory, as documented in these human patients with global amnesia, which demonstrates the importance of this brain region in forming declarative memories and for consolidating long-term memories out of short-term memories.

SPECIFIC BRAIN SYSTEMS AND LEARNING

The hippocampus and the neighboring structures of the limbic system are one example of a specific memory system that is

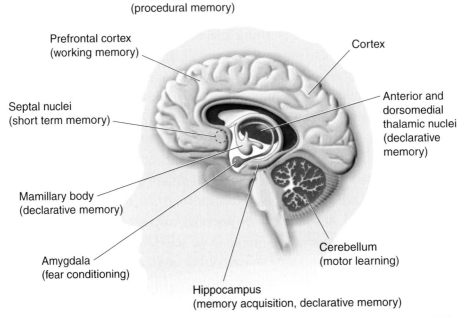

Striatum (not shown)
(procedural memory)

Prefrontal cortex
(working memory)

Cortex

Septal nuclei
(short term memory)

Anterior and
dorsomedial
thalamic nuclei
(declarative
memory)

Mamillary body
(declarative memory)

Amygdala
(fear conditioning)

Cerebellum
(motor learning)

Hippocampus
(memory acquisition, declarative memory)

Figure 5.3 The limbic system includes the cortex surrounding the temporal lobe and several structures buried beneath the cortex, including the amygdala, hippocampus, and thalamus. The limbic system is connected to virtually every part of the brain.

localized to specific regions of the brain. In studies of brain lesions in animal models, the cerebellum has proven critical for motor skills and procedural memories. A simple procedural task, the eye-blink response, occurs when a puff of air is applied to the eye. The eye-blink reflex can be classically conditioned to a tone, as described in Chapter 3. The timing of the learned eye-blink response can be altered or lost completely by specific lesions in the cerebellum. Another motor skill regulated by the cerebellum is the vestibulo-ocular reflex, an automatic movement of the eye that attempts to compensate for movements of the head. The relevant circuitry of both the eye-blink response and the vestibulo-ocular reflex have been sufficiently defined, so that extremely small lesions in the brain can produce dramatic losses in these behaviors. These studies demonstrate that animal learning and memory can replicate human behavioral deficits and generate new findings to advance our understanding of the distribution and localization of learning and memory in the brain.

SUMMARY

Researchers have long sought to identify the structures in the brain that are the site for memory formation and storage. To this end, considerable study has been undertaken to locate the memory engram, believed to be the biological basis of memory in the brain.

Early efforts to locate the memory engram involved localizing the areas in the brain responsible for learning and memory. Particularly significant were the animal model studies performed by Karl Lashley in the 1920s. Lashley examined the effects of selectively induced brain damage on maze-learning in rats. From these experiments, Lashley concluded that no specific region of the brain is essential to long-term memory, and that memory is distributed throughout the brain.

Lashley's studies demonstrated that memory formation and storage are more complex and distributed than previously believed, but also underscored some important limitations on animal models of learning and memory. The animals used in experiments cannot describe the cognitive processes or sensory cues they use to perform a task. This forces the researcher to make assumptions about what processes or cues are responsible for the observed behaviors, leaving open the possibility of misinterpreting the results.

Research into learning and memory in humans has the advantage of experimental subjects who can describe the task-performing strategies they use. Human behavioral research is limited, however, by the tendency of human subjects to inaccurately describe their behavioral strategies, and also by ethical constraints that prohibit direct manipulation and modification of healthy brain tissue. Patients who have suffered brain damage from injury or disease provide the opportunity to examine learning and memory in the human brain. A particularly noteworthy example of this is H. M., a male patient who in 1953 underwent experimental brain surgery for the treatment of debilitating epilepsy. The surgery was largely effective in treating the epilepsy and also produced effects that proved highly revealing about the processes and mechanisms of human memory.

Evaluations of H. M. and other patients with brain damage have revealed that there are certain structures in the brain that are essential to the processes of memory formation, storage, and retrieval. These structures, which include the amygdala, hippocampus, and hypothalamus, are known collectively as the limbic system. Other areas of the brain that play key roles to particular aspects of memory—for example, the cerebellum, which is essential to procedural memory—have also been identified.

■ **Learn more about the brain's organization of memory** Search the Internet for *memory engram*, *Santiago Ramón y Cajal*, or *Karl Lashley*.

6 | Molecular Mechanisms of Learning and Memory

PROTEINS: DEFINING AND REGULATING CELL FUNCTION

In addition to seeking the brain structures important for learning and memory, researchers have sought to identify the chemicals and molecules that regulate learning and memory. Researchers are particularly interested in small biologically active molecules called **second messengers** and the **proteins** they activate. Proteins serve a variety of important functions in the body, and there may be as many as 50,000 proteins in the body. Many second messengers and proteins are active in regulatory pathways and signaling networks, which makes the quest to understand the molecular mechanisms of learning and memory the neurobiological equivalent of finding a needle in a haystack.

Proteins are made up of specific sequences of the 20 **amino acids** present in our bodies. The amino acid sequence of each protein is responsible for giving the protein its structure and function, and is dictated by specific DNA sequences called genes (Figure 6.1). To define what proteins do in cells is a bit like defining what words do for language. You cannot have language without words, and you cannot have cells without proteins. DNA defines the genetic potential of any organism, but it is the proteins that the DNA codes for that

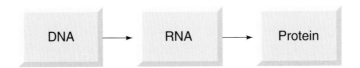

Figure 6.1 The flow of genetic information travels from DNA to RNA to proteins.

permit the DNA to replicate, divide, or accomplish any of the myriad of tasks that each and every cell in your body performs. Proteins are part of the hemoglobin in your red blood cells that transport oxygen from your lungs to the rest of your body. Proteins include the collagen that makes your skin soft and supple, yet durable. Proteins also make up the enzymes in your body that turn seemingly unlikely chemical reactions into highly productive, life-sustaining processes.

Experiments that have successfully advanced our understanding of the molecular mechanisms of learning and memory have used three main strategies:

1. Pharmacological inhibition of a protein or family of proteins to block a learned behavior.
2. Identification of proteins without an initial bias that are active or that have increased abundance during learning and memory.
3. Manipulation of an organism's DNA to eliminate or increase a specific protein's function.

PHARMACOLOGICAL INTERFERENCE WITH MEMORY

The rationale for using small molecules, such as cell-permeable chemicals, is to reduce the activity or level of one or more proteins to interfere with the molecular mechanisms of learning and memory. This approach is similar to the strategy employed by Lashley (see Chapter 5), who destroyed specific areas of a rodent's brain to determine if learning and memory was affected. Pharmacological inhibitors are used to produce lesions in specific areas of an organism's nervous system. The main problem of this approach is identifying which protein to inhibit.

In the mid-1960s, Swedish neurobiologist Holger Hyden reported that the level of enzymes in the neurons of the brain increased following brain activity. Hyden believed that this was a consequence of increased levels of RNA in the neurons after neuronal activity. Researchers at Abbott Laboratories in Illinois tested Hyden's theory and reported that magnesium pemoline (trade name: Cylert®) enhanced learning and memory in rodents, presumably by increasing RNA synthesis in neurons. Since the late 1960s, Cylert (now called pemoline) has been used successfully to treat complex neurological disorders, including attention-deficit/hyperactivity disorder (ADHD) and sleep disorders (see "Neuroscience and the Media" box).

In the 1960s, Hyden, the Abbott group, and others examined the role of RNA in learning and memory, but the role of increased protein synthesis—a logical consequence of increased RNA levels—remained a mystery. To explore the connection between protein synthesis and learning and memory, Bernard Agranoff and his colleagues at the University of Michigan performed experiments in classical conditioning with goldfish.

Like Pavlov's dogs, goldfish can be classically conditioned in an **avoidance assay** (**test**). Rather than building an association between food and a bell as Pavlov did, Agranoff and his colleagues conditioned goldfish to associate an electric shock with a flash of light. A light source was paired with an electric shock that the goldfish could avoid by immediately crossing a barrier and moving to the other side of the aquarium. Fish readily learned to avoid the shock and quickly demonstrated a high probability of moving to the other side of the aquarium in response to the light.

To test long-term memory, Agranoff waited hours (or even days) and tested trained fish to see if the goldfish retained any memory of their prior training (Figure 6.2). If the fish had any long-term memory of the learned behavior, the percentage of avoided shocks hours (or days) after training would be similar to the percentage immediately after training. Agranoff reasoned that injection of a protein synthesis inhibitor—in this experiment, the antibiotic puromycin—would block learning and memory if protein synthesis was important for these processes.

Neuroscience and the Media

Mechanisms of learning and memory are as attractive to the media today as they were in 1961 when *Time* magazine highlighted Swedish neurobiologist Holger Hyden's discoveries in an article titled "The Chemistry of Thought" and in 1966, when *Time* described Abbott Laboratories' discoveries in "A Molecule for Memory." Central to Hyden's theories was the concept that neuronal activity produced specific patterns of RNA, which formed a molecular imprint of memory. In its article, *Time* used scientific buzzwords such as *mind, computer, RNA, memory, neuron, thought control*, and *brainwashing* to make Hyden's theories attractive to the general public. Current theories do not support Hyden's concept that individual neurons possess unique memories via specific patterns of RNA. Rather, converging evidence suggests that memory is a natural outcome of multiple brain systems and that the fundamental unit of memory is not contained within an individual neuron, but in multiple neurons that form distinct yet functionally connected circuits. Hyden's theory for the importance of RNA in memory, however, was on target, as later research clearly demonstrated that the formation of new proteins is essential for the formation of long-term memories.

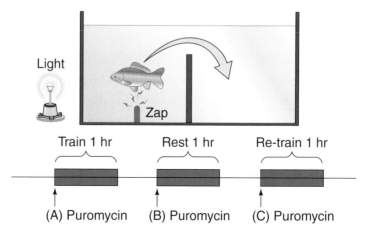

Figure 6.2 When a light was turned on, the fish learned that the only way to avoid shock was to swim to the other side of the aquarium. Puromycin was given at different times during the training to test the effects of inhibiting protein synthesis on learning and memory.

When puromycin was injected into fish that had already undergone training several hours before, no change in the learned behavior was observed. Agranoff concluded that puromycin injection (or the manipulation of the fish to inject the drug into its skull) after a behavior was learned did not prevent recall of the learned behavior (i.e., memory) nor did it disrupt the swim behavior itself (i.e., alter performance). Agranoff was now ready to test whether puromycin adversely affected learning and memory. To do this, Agranoff decided to test whether puromycin injection immediately after the fish was successfully trained in the avoidance assay (rather than several hours later, as described above) altered the learned behavior. Injecting the fish with puromycin immediately after training blocked any memory of the avoidance training when the fish was retested days or even hours after training. Significantly, fish that received puromycin immediately *before* training displayed normal learning behavior; however, when these fish were retested days later, they appeared not to recall the learned behavior. These experiments demonstrated that puromycin injection does not block acquisition of the avoidance assay, indicating that protein synthesis is not required for short-term memory. The fact that long-term memory acquisition was prevented by puromycin treatment indicates that transition of the learned behavior from short-term to long-term memory, however, does require protein synthesis. Finally, once the learned behavior has been moved into long-term memory, it no longer requires protein synthesis.

To date, several different protein synthesis inhibitors have been used to demonstrate the universality of protein synthesis in long-term memory. This observation has been established in a number of organisms, including fish, worms, insects, birds, rodents, and primates. One explanation for the role of protein synthesis in long-term memory is that long-term memory requires neuronal growth, or changes in the shape or number of neuronal contacts (synapses). It is believed that this growth or change increases the efficiency of the communication between neurons. Unlike long-term memory, short-term memory does not appear to require additional protein resources or neuronal growth. As we discuss in Chapters 7 and 8, immediate changes (such as activation of key second messenger pathways and specific proteins) affect the connectivity of neurons by rapid and reversible mechanisms that do not require protein synthesis.

GENETIC DISSECTION OF MEMORY

Pharmacological interference is a powerful strategy for defining the molecular mechanisms of learning and memory. It is limited, however, by the fact that chemical inhibitors often lack specificity. For example, the antibiotic anisomycin potently blocks protein synthesis and has been shown in animal studies to block long-term memory when injected immediately after training—much as puromycin did in Agranoff's experiments. In addition to blocking protein synthesis, however, anisomycin also activates a family of stress-activated proteins called mitogen-activated protein kinases (MAP kinases), which are regulatory molecules that are also thought to play a role in learning and memory. It is unclear, therefore, whether anisomycin blocks long-term memory because it inhibits protein synthesis, activates MAP kinases, or both. Genetic approaches to the study of learning and memory rely on the introduction of specific alterations to the genome of an organism. The lack of specificity inherent to small molecule inhibitors is, therefore, not an issue.

The role of an organism's genetics to shape its **phenotype** comes from long-standing biological traditions. From the observations on natural selection by naturalist Charles Darwin (1809–1882) to the conclusions drawn about plant variability by geneticist Gregor Mendel (1822–1884), our current understanding of biology is built on the concept that genes are central to an organism's function. In the latter part of the 20th century, an experimental approach that gained prominence was the application of **forward genetics** to explore the complex properties of the brain—including learning and memory. In this approach, researchers use radiation or chemicals to produce random **mutations** (changes in genetic information) in an organism's **genome**, and then observe any resulting changes in behavior. The goal is to associate specific deficits in learning and memory with the genes responsible for producing them.

FORWARD GENETIC STRATEGIES IN LEARNING AND MEMORY

The fruit fly is an organism that is commonly used to identify genes involved with learning and memory using **forward genetics**. The **genetic screen** is the process of examining thousands of different mutations to find a specific phenotype (the observable effect of a gene; in this case, a behavior). One challenging aspect of using forward genetics is producing an assay (test) to study learning and memory that permits the researcher to examine many mutants at once. The fruit fly *Drosophila* performs non-associative and associative tasks quite easily. One assay used to illustrate classical conditioning in fruit flies is based on pairing a particular odor with an electric shock. Like Agranoff's fish and Pavlov's dogs, fruit flies quickly learn to associate an initially neutral stimulus (i.e., odor) with an unpleasant outcome, like a shock. After repeated exposures to the odor and shock, the flies are tested in a T-maze—a T-shaped glass or plastic enclosure that permits the researcher to determine the effectiveness of training based on where the flies move in response to a particular stimulus. For example, if the odor paired with the shock is presented on the left arm of the T-maze, normal flies will almost always choose to move to the right arm. Once the behavioral assay is established, the researcher produces mutations in the flies' genomes (ideally, producing one gene mutation per fly), and then screens the flies for a specific behavioral phenotype (i.e., flies that cannot learn the odor-aversion task). Lethal mutations, such as those that deform the wings or eliminate the flies' ability to detect odors, are not usable phenotypes in studies of behavior. Thus, in addition to being screened in the odor-avoidance assay, all of the mutant flies are also tested for their relative performance at "being a fly"—for example, their ability to fly and to smell.

A number of learning and memory mutants have been identified in fruit flies. The first was aptly named *dunce* (see "The Scientific Naming of Fruit Fly Mutants" box). The dunce mutant demonstrates normal sensory (i.e., smell) and motor function (i.e., flying) yet possesses severe deficits in learning. Tests to evaluate the formation of long-term versus short-term memories revealed that dunce's ability to form short-term memory was reduced and that it had little ability to establish new long-term memories. Further examination indicated that previous long-term memories established by dunce degraded at a rate similar to normal flies. This suggests that dunce's reduced ability to maintain short-term memories contributes to its inability to form new long-term memories. The dunce mutant has a specific mutation in the gene that encodes for an enzyme called cyclic AMP (**cAMP**) phosphodiesterase. This enzyme is important for destroying ("hydrolyzing") cAMP and is significantly elevated in dunce flies compared to normal flies (we discuss the relationship of cAMP and protein signaling in Chapters 7 and 8).

What does cAMP do, where does it come from, and why is it important for learning and memory? cAMP is produced by another enzyme in response to specific cellular cues associated with neuronal activity. cAMP is considered a second messenger

The Scientific Naming of Fruit Fly Mutants

The names for *Drosophila* fruit fly mutants may have begun with a strict sense of nomenclature, as in the white-eyes mutant termed *white*. Since that time, choosing names for the mutant flies has evolved into something of an art form. Unlike most scientific disciplines that tend to use the name of the people who make the discoveries, neuroscience has used delightful if not comical names to identify memory mutants of *Drosophila*. For example, *dunce* and *amnesiac* are accurate in their description of the inability of these flies to learn. Mutant flies with dysfunctional learning have also been named after vegetables (i.e., *rutabaga*, *cabbage*, and *turnip*), presumably to refer to their vegetable-like intellect. Another naming strategy employed by fruit fly neurobiologists is to name mutant flies after Pavlov's dogs. This task required that fruit fly researcher Tim Tully travel to Pavlov's home to search through his research notebooks to find the names of his favorite dogs. See *http://tinman.vetmed.helsinki.fi/eng/drosophila.html* for further names of fruit fly mutants and their origins.

because it activates another enzyme, cAMP-dependent protein kinase (PKA). Once activated, PKA can regulate the activity and function of many other proteins through a rapid and reversible modification, termed **phosphorylation**. Thus, under specific conditions, neuronal activity is associated with an increase in cAMP levels, which, in turn, leads to the activation of PKA and the regulation of its target proteins. This suggests that one or many of these target proteins in the neuron that are regulated by PKA may be the molecular signal that leads to learning and memory. The universality of cAMP signaling and its role in learning and memory was further validated when additional fly mutants, which all displayed defective short-term and long-term memory, were serendipitously found to have mutations in others genes that were all related to cAMP signaling.

REVERSE GENETIC STRATEGIES IN LEARNING AND MEMORY

Forward genetic approaches work best in organisms that reproduce rapidly and are easily studied in large numbers, such as fish, nematode worms, and fruit flies. Forward genetics can also be applied to more complex organisms like rodents, although the slower reproduction rates and difficulty of studying hundreds or thousands of mutants at a time make this approach more difficult. The larger genomes of mammals make it necessary to study many more mutants to successfully identify genes related to learning and memory.

When a mutant with deficient learning and memory is found, the gene that caused the mutation must be identified to determine the protein product it produces, and then retested to confirm its role in learning and memory. For example, even in a simple organism such as the nematode worm *Caenorhabditis elegans*, which has 302 neurons (humans have 100 billion neurons), the genome is large enough that it is still difficult to locate and identify the mutated gene. Fortunately, by the end of the

20th century, a new technology that could target specific genes in an organism's genome, **reverse genetics**, was developed. Reverse genetics has been highly successful even in complex organisms like rodents because of the development of a technology called **transgenics**. Using transgenics, a researcher alters a germinal cell of an embryo so that the DNA of a specific gene is mutated to block the production of a particular protein. The offspring of the transgenic subject may inherit the mutation because it is passed from generation to generation in the genetic material.

One of the first transgenic organisms used to study learning and memory was a mouse produced by Alcino Silva, a neurobiologist working with the Noble laureate Susumu Tonegawa at the Massachusetts Institute of Technology (MIT). Silva's transgenic mouse was deficient in a particular enzyme (calcium-calmodulin-dependent protein kinase II, or CaMKII). CaMKII had been previously implicated in regulating neuronal signaling using inhibitor molecules such as described above for classical interference studies. An organism lacking a specific protein because it has been genetically altered is termed a *knockout* (because the gene was "knocked out"). Silva found that the CaMKII knockout was not able to learn spatial relationships and memory tasks and, as we will discuss in Chapter 8, did not possess a form of synaptic plasticity in the hippocampus termed *long-term potentiation.*

A complication of the reverse genetic approach is that knockout could adversely affect development. Because the target gene is silenced at birth, it is difficult to determine whether the inability of the mice to learn a particular task is due to dysfunctional learning and memory or because of developmental abnormalities inherited at birth. Recent advances have attempted to specifically address such concerns by producing more sophisticated knockout approaches. One approach, termed **inducible knockout**, uses technology that permits the researcher to silence a gene at any time, typically well after the animal's birth. Research into ways of refining this technique—and of localizing targeted genes to specific regions of the nervous system, rather than simply throughout the entire brain or body of an organism—is ongoing.

CORRELATING MOLECULES WITH MEMORY

The **correlative approach** to studying the molecular mechanisms of learning and memory does not have the specificity that is associated with the interference and genetic approaches. It is more general than the interference and genetic approaches because the researcher simply tries to correlate all of the proteins that change (in level or activity) during learning and memory. The drawback of correlating a large number of potential candidate proteins with learning and memory is that these proteins must then be identified and retested using the interference or genetic approaches to determine their specificity and function. Recent advances in **proteomics** is permitting researchers to monitor changes in the level, function, or localization of many proteins at once. This new **high-throughput approach** is an important addition to correlative studies because it enables researchers to quickly identify new candidate proteins implicated in learning and memory, thus increasing the speed and efficiency of the genetic and interference approaches. Proteomics also permits researchers to look at protein networks. The function of individual proteins may only be important relative to their

Signaling Networks in Learning and Memory

Groups of neurons linked through specific functions form neural networks. The anatomical and cellular basis of learning and memory is produced by networks of neurons that make up systems in the brain (e.g., the limbic system). Proteins also form functionally related signaling groups. Therefore, the phrase *protein network* is used to describe complex interactions involving multiple proteins.

relationship to the other proteins within a given protein network (see "Signaling Networks in Learning and Memory" box). The ability to study protein networks may be the most important contribution of proteomics, because the interactions and communications of protein signaling networks can only be studied using techniques that permit analysis of many proteins at the same time.

SUMMARY

The role of certain chemicals and molecules in learning and memory is of keen interest to researchers. In particular, the contribution of proteins to these processes has been the subject of considerable study. Three main approaches (or a combination of these) have been used to identify the proteins involved with learning and memory.

The interference approach makes use of pharmacological inhibitors to interfere with a learned behavior. The limitation of this approach is uncertainty over whether the inhibitors are specific to the target protein being studied.

The genetic approach involves the modification of an organism's genetic makeup to alter the activity of specific proteins. This approach is highly specific in that the protein of interest can be directly studied through a lesion or up-regulation of its gene. The primary limitation of the genetic approach is that unwanted secondary changes associated with abnormal development of the nervous system confound the analysis.

The third approach is the correlative approach, in which changes in the activity or level of proteins during learning and memory are assessed. The limitation of this approach is that it is difficult to determine whether the change in the protein is necessary for learning or memory or whether it is simply correlated to, or a by-product of, the behavior.

■ **Learn more about the role of proteins in learning and memory**
Search the Internet for *proteins* and *learning and memory*.

7 An Invertebrate Model of Learning and Memory

LEARNING AND MEMORY IN INVERTEBRATES

Many model systems have been developed in simple organisms to study the molecular and cellular mechanisms of learning and memory. In particular, invertebrates (e.g., worms, insects, mollusks) have fewer neurons and much simpler nervous systems than vertebrates (Figure 7.1). Invertebrates can learn to perform most of the various forms of learning discussed in Chapter 3. For example, snails, slugs, and nematode worms all demonstrate nonassociative forms of learning, such as habituation, dishabituation, and sensitization. These invertebrates also display more complex forms of learning, such as associative conditioning. The trick to studying learning in invertebrates lies in designing the appropriate task to examine a learned behavior. For example, all invertebrates can modify their feeding behaviors. The terrestrial mollusk *Limax* moves toward desirable food odors, a response that can be inhibited by noxious chemicals or shock. Other forms of learning studied in invertebrates often take advantage of the organism's natural behavior to escape a predator, for example, the "tail-flip" behavior in crayfish and the swim response of the nudibranch *Triontia*. Below we examine the cellular and molecular details that produce nonassociative learning in the marine mollusk *Aplysia*.

(A)

(B)

Figure 7.1 *Limax* **(A)**, *Tritonia* **(B)**, and *Aplysia* **(C)** (see next page) have simple nervous systems, yet still display complex behaviors related to feeding, tactile stimulation, and escape responses. These attributes have made these invertebrates instrumental in identifying molecular and cellular mechanisms of learning and memory.

(C)

Figure 7.1 *(continued)*

THE MARINE MOLLUSK *APLYSIA*

Extensive use of the marine mollusk *Aplysia* in neuroscientific research began in the 1960s and was pioneered by Columbia University neuroscientist Eric Kandel (in 2000, Kandel was awarded the Nobel Prize in Medicine for his work in discovering key molecular mechanisms of learning and memory). The nervous system of *Aplysia* consists of 18,000–20,000 neurons. The brain of *Aplysia* is organized into discrete groups of nerve cells, or ganglia (singular is *ganglion*): four pairs of head ganglia and one abdominal ganglion. Kandel and his colleagues believed that the nervous systems of organisms—whether they have 20,000 neurons or 100 billion neurons—share similar mechanisms for learning.

Kandel and his colleagues took advantage of the following observations about the neurons that made up the nervous system of *Aplysia:*

1. They are small in number.
2. They are functionally localized to specific ganglia.
3. They are relatively invariant in location and appearance.
4. They are large in diameter (up to 1 mm—roughly 10–20 times larger than human neurons).

These attributes suggested that if specific behaviors could be defined in *Aplysia*, it would be possible to experimentally dissect learning and memory using a multidisciplinary approach, combining molecular and behavioral perspectives along with biophysical and cellular analysis.

What behavior should be studied in an animal that lies around all day, presumably "thinking" about little more than seaweed and reproduction? Ocean creatures, like land organisms, must react to their environment to survive. A defensive or escape reflex could be observed following stimulation to the siphon (a tube-shaped organ that permits an organism to take in or expel water). The withdrawal of both the gill and siphon is a reflex that likely evolved to simultaneously protect these fleshy organs from damage. Stimulating the siphon with a light stream of water habituated the withdrawal reflex, whereas a noxious stimulus (like a shock or pinch) produced sensitization of the reflex. Thus, *Aplysia* displays stereotypical forms of nonassociative learning: Siphon stimulation can be modified to enhance or inhibit this withdrawal reflex (see Chapter 3).

To identify the molecular and cellular changes that accompany nonassociative learning, Kandel and his colleagues used a series of reductive steps (i.e., understanding the behavior in components rather than as an entire process) in conjunction with attempts to simplify the experimental preparation with each new piece of information. For example, once the gill-siphon withdrawal reflex could be manipulated in an open preparation of *Aplysia*, the next step was to isolate a functional gill-siphon reflex from a dissected animal using only the gill/siphon and abdominal ganglia. Although the reduced preparation was more accessible to biophysical manipulation of the neurons using **whole-cell recording** and **electrophysiology** than using the intact animal, researchers still had to identify which sensory neurons in the abdominal ganglia terminated in the skin and responded to touch and which motor neurons in the abdominal ganglia terminated on the muscles of the gill and siphon to drive muscle contraction.

Mechanical stimulation of the skin around the siphon revealed 24 neurons that were responsive to touch. Direct stimulation of the neurons in the abdominal ganglia showed that a population of 13 motor neurons made direct contacts with the gill/siphon muscles.

A population of interneurons (nerve cells that do not form direct connections with sensory endings or muscle, and only connect to other neurons) in the abdominal ganglia that did not make direct connections on the muscle cells or receive sensory information was also found. These interneurons appeared to make excitatory (activating) or inhibitory (deactivating) contacts on the motor neurons within the ganglia. Identification of the connections between sensory, motor, and interneurons permitted the researchers to examine which components of the neural circuit for the gill/siphon withdrawal reflex changed during learning, as well as the molecular mechanisms that were responsible for these changes in neuronal function (Figure 7.2).

Nonassociative learning (sensitization) appears to occur at the cellular level through changes in the firing properties of the sensory neurons onto their motor neurons. This process appears to result from changes in the membrane properties of the sensory neurons and the synaptic efficacy of their contacts on motor neurons. In other words, sensitization is an increase in the responsiveness of a behavior, like enhanced gill/siphon withdrawal following a strong stimulus. This increase is medi-ated at the cellular level by changes in the properties of the

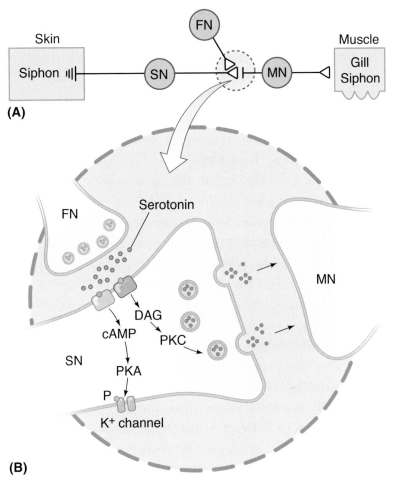

(A)

(B)

Figure 7.2 A diagram of the neuronal connections and the molecular changes that underlie the gill/siphon withdrawal reflex in *Aplysia*. **(A)** Stimulus to the siphon skin activates the sensory neurons (SN) which synapse onto the motor neurons (MN) that retract the gill/siphon. The neuronal "wiring" diagram illustrates the basic connectivity for the gill/ siphon withdrawal. At the cellular level, sensitization of the gill/siphon withdrawal reflex is produced when a strong stimulus recruits the acti- vation of facilitatory (FN) neurons, which modulate the strength of the SN synapse onto the MN. **(B)** At the molecular level, strengthening of the SN synapse onto the MN is due to the release of serotonin by the FN neuron onto the SN neuron. Activation of serotonin receptors ele- vates key second messengers, cAMP and DAG, which function to acti- vate protein kinases (PKA and PKC).

sensory neurons that activate the motor neuron and produce retraction of the gill/siphon. But what changes at the molecular level are responsible for this enhanced ability of the sensory neuron to activate the motor neurons?

Sensitization of the siphon-gill withdrawal reflex results from a brief exposure to a noxious stimulus, such as a shock to the siphon, which produces short-term sensitization (i.e., lasting minutes to hours). The noxious stimulus, in this case a brief electrical shock, results in the release of modulatory neurotransmitters (e.g., serotonin) from a subtype of interneurons called facilitatory interneurons. Activation of the facilitatory interneurons by a strong stimulus causes the release of serotonin onto the sensory neuron. Activation of the facilitatory interneuron increases the probability that subsequent stimuli received by the sensory neuron result in activation of the motor neuron. The action of serotonin on the sensory neuron appears to result from its binding to a specific receptor (i.e., serotonin receptor) in the plasma membrane of the sensory neuron, which is associated with the stimulation of **adenylyl cyclase**, a protein that increases the cellular level of **cAMP**. Second messengers can be ions like calcium or small molecules like cAMP and **DAG** that trigger a biochemical reaction inside the cell in response to events occurring outside the cell—in this case, the release of serotonin caused by the shock and its subsequent binding to the serotonin receptor signals for increased cAMP and DAG production. As an enzyme product, cAMP is produced in high levels in the cell. This functions to amplify the transduction of the stimulus, which produces global changes in the biochemical environment of the cell. For example, cAMP activates a protein kinase, cAMP-dependent protein kinase (PKA), which further amplifies the signal by regulating the activity of a number of different proteins through **phosphorylation**. The cAMP signal is reduced or turned off by **hydrolyzation** of cAMP via the action of **phosphodiesterases**, proteins that reduce cAMP levels and terminate the signal of this second messenger. A reduction in cAMP causes PKA to inactivate, and through the action of **phosphatases**, the phosphorylated substrates return to their normal activity after **dephosphorylation**. Activation of the sensory neuron is also associated with an elevation in intracellular calcium levels. DAG is analogous to cAMP, in that as a second messenger it functions to trigger a biochemical reaction inside the cell in response to external stimuli. One protein DAG activates is **PKC**, a multifunctional protein kinase that, like PKA, phosphorylates specific substrates to enhance synaptic transmission.

In short-term sensitization, the signaling cascade from serotonin to an elevation in cAMP and activation of PKA terminates on specific PKA substrate proteins that are important for regulating the ability of sensory neurons to activate motor neurons. Protein substrates of PKA act at multiple levels in the sensory neuron to facilitate motor neuron firing. For example, PKA phosphorylates potassium channel in the sensory neuron's plasma membrane. Serotonin binding slows repolarization of the cell by inhibiting the opening of the channel. This extends the action potential in the sensory neuron to facilitate the release of neurotransmitters onto the motor neuron. Thus, the sensory neuron is better able to activate the motor neuron because it is now releasing more neurotransmitter.

What about long-term sensitization? If the signaling from serotonin to PKA activation is all reversed by the action of phosphatases, a logical question is: How do repeated exposures of a noxious stimulus result in long-term sensitization (i.e., lasting days to weeks)? It appears that long-term and short-term sensitization initially share common molecular mechanisms (i.e., serotonin to cAMP to PKA) except that for a long-term effect, repeated exposure to the noxious stimulus resulting in gene transcription and protein synthesis is required. Repeated exposures to the noxious stimulus results in PKA translocation to the nucleus, where one substrate of PKA (the transcription factor CREB) is poised to turn on gene transcription following its phosphorylation. Although this is only a brief description of the process, current estimates indicate that at least a dozen proteins have increased synthesis in response to CREB activation, including proteins that feed back to facilitate activation of PKA and proteins that permit structural rearrangements in the terminals of the sensory neurons. Both mechanisms would enhance or potentiate the ability of the sensory neuron to activate the motor neuron. These data also suggest that no one protein is *the* long-term memory molecule, but rather the accumulated effect of multiple proteins that all function to increase the responsiveness of the sensory neuron and its ability to drive the motor neuron.

SUMMARY

Because they have simpler nervous systems and can display different forms of learning, invertebrates have been used in the study of the molecular and cellular mechanisms of learning and memory. Since the 1960s, the siphon withdrawal reflex of the marine mollusk *Aplysia* has been studied extensively as a model of learning and memory.

In studies examining the siphon withdrawal response of *Aplysia*, researchers have identified the sensory neurons that are responsive to touch and the motor neurons that initiate muscle contraction. They have also identified interneurons that exert modulatory effects on the sensory and motor neurons. Through analysis of the changes that occurred in these neurons and interneurons during learning, researchers have gained insight into the molecular mechanisms of the learning process. Specifically, they determined that sensitization represents an increased responsiveness to a strong stimulus, and that this increased responsiveness appears to result from changes at the cellular level in the sensory neurons that result in their having an increased probability of firing a motor neuron to any given stimulus. These cellular changes are induced by specific biochemical responses inside the sensory neuron in response to the neurotransmitter serotonin, which is released from a certain type of facilitatory interneuron.

The researchers found the mechanisms of short-term and long-term sensitization to be largely similar biochemical responses, with the notable difference that long-term sensitization resulting from repeated exposure to the stimulus in question requires protein synthesis.

■ **Learn more about research on learning and memory in invertebrates** Search the Internet for *invertebrate* and *brain*.

Long-Term Potentiation: A Synaptic Correlate of Learning and Memory

SYNAPTIC PLASTICITY IN LEARNING

In the simplest terms, plasticity describes the capacity of an organism to be altered or molded. Neuronal connections are continually being sculpted. Development, experience, and even injury can alter an organism's neural circuits. **Synaptic plasticity** refers to the continual change in the connectivity of neurons. In the previous chapter, we discussed the plasticity of the synapses between sensory and motor neurons, and how it underlies sensitization of the gill/siphon withdrawal reflex in *Aplysia*. The ability to modify even this simple behavior appears to require numerous neuronal interactions (i.e., sensory, motor, and interneurons) and biochemical responses to alter the cellular behavior of individual neurons. Identifying the cellular and molecular mechanisms responsible for this defensive reflex in *Aplysia* was made much easier by the fact that the neurons of the nervous system of mollusks are localized to specific ganglia—in this case, the abdominal ganglion. The vertebrate brain is considerably more complex than the ganglia of invertebrates, which makes the study of the cellular and molecular mechanisms underlying learning and memory in vertebrates difficult to isolate, much less elucidate.

One approach used to study learning and memory in vertebrates has been to study the molecular and cellular mechanisms of synaptic plasticity in the absence of a definable behavioral component. In other words, researchers target the molecular mechanisms that produce cellular changes believed to underlie learning and memory. One such change is **long-term potentiation** (**LTP**), an activity-dependent form of synaptic plasticity that is analogous in many ways to the cellular changes observed in the abdominal ganglion of *Aplysia* after sensitization. LTP is typically studied in the hippocampus, a part of the limbic system that is essential for spatial memory and moving information from short-term to long-term memory (see Chapter 5). As we discuss below, LTP functions at the cellular level to strengthen the synaptic connections between neurons and recapitulates many of the molecular and cellular changes important for invertebrate learning and memory.

HIPPOCAMPAL LTP: A FORM OF ACTIVITY-DEPENDENT PLASTICITY

Researchers initially chose to target the hippocampus to look for long-term changes in synaptic strength because this region was previously shown to be important for learning and memory in humans (see Chapter 5). The hippocampus resembles the curved shape of a seahorse and resides within the temporal lobes (see Chapter 1). The hippocampus is divided into three main regions: CA3, CA2, and CA1. **Pyramidal neurons** make up the CA3-CA1 regions. The circuitry of the hippocampus is designed so that as information in the form of neuronal activity is received in the hippocampus, it is processed and then passed back into the cortex. Specifically, neuronal activity from the cortex enters the hippocampus at the level of the **granule cells** in the dentate gyrus. From there, the neuronal activity is propagated into the CA3 neurons, where is passes among the CA2 and CA1 neurons before it returns to the cortex. It is not possible to associate specific behaviors with a given neuron or small group of neurons in the hippocampus. As with the connections exhibited within the *Aplysia* ganglia, however, the neurons of the hippocampus make stereotypical excitatory connections throughout the hippocampus, which makes possible the study of intact neuronal circuits, either in a living animal or in sections excised from the brain.

In the early 1970s, Bliss and Lomo at the University of Oslo, showed that multiple action potentials (called a high frequency tetanus), produced long-lasting changes in the strength of hippocampal synaptic connections. Specifically, in anesthetized rabbits, stimulation of the perforant pathway (i.e., axons from the cortex that synapse on the granule neurons of the dentate gyrus) with a brief but rapid train of action potentials (100s per second) produced a long-lasting enhancement in the strength of these connections. This increase in synaptic efficacy, termed long-term potentiation (LTP), can persist for several weeks (Figure 8.1).

THE CELLULAR PROPERTIES OF HIPPOCAMPAL LTP

Long-term potentiation was first demonstrated by T. V. Bliss and T. Lomo in 1973; however, the concept that memory was encoded through changes in the synaptic strength between active neurons was proposed at the turn of the 20th century by Santigao Ramón y Cajal (see Chapter 2) and later by Donald Hebb, a physiologist-psychologist at McGill University, in a 1949 book entitled, *The Organization of Behavior: A Neuropsychological Theory.*

The subject of LTP as *the* cellular device for learning and memory has been intensely studied and hotly debated over the past 30 years. In fact, the increased focus on neuroscience as a field during the latter part of the 20th century began as a movement in the 1990s known as the decade of the brain. This era could also have been described as the decade of LTP (See the "Long-Term Potentiation" box.)

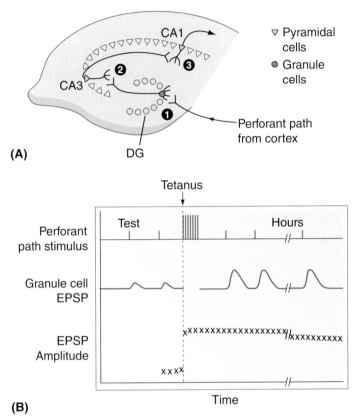

Figure 8.1 A diagram illustrating long-term potentiation (LTP) in the hippocampus. **(A)** A slice through the hippocampus reveals the neuronal circuitry where LTP has been studied, including the perforant pathway onto the granule cells (1), the granule cells onto CA3 neurons (2), and CA3 neurons onto CA1 pyramidal cells (3). **(B)** Granule cell excitatory post-synaptic potentials measured after high frequency stimulation (i.e., tetanus) reveal an increase in the amplitude of the excitatory post-synaptic potential that persists for hours to days.

MOLECULAR MECHANISMS OF HIPPOCAMPAL LTP

Electrophysiological dissection of LTP in slices of hippocampal tissue has revealed details about the time-course in the development and molecular requirements to produce this change. LTP in these samples was found to require high frequency (100 Hz or 100 per second) stimulation. Indeed, stimulation for the same number of times, but at a slower frequency (1 Hz or 1 per second), produces a phenomenon called **long-term depression** (**LTD**). The existence of LTD was an important finding: The implication that LTP is a long-term synaptic modification makes conceivable the idea that a one-way change in synaptic strength could saturate all of the synapses throughout the lifetime of an organism. The ability to decrease the activity of a synapse permits two-way regulation of synaptic strength. The potential to increase, decrease, and—importantly—reverse alterations in synaptic strength by different patterns of neuronal activity was one of the fundamental findings in 20th century neuroscience (see "The Hippocampal Slice Preparation" box).

The first clue in the search for the molecular mechanisms of LTP can be found in the role of high-frequency stimulation in producing this phenomenon. For the case of LTP measured at the CA1 neurons, the high-frequency stimulus of the axons that synapse onto the dendritic fields of the CA1 pyramidal neurons (see synapse 3; Figure 8.1A), produces a strong depolarization that is essential for LTP (Figure 8.2). Electrophysiological methods have been used to show that if the CA1 pyramidal neurons are prevented from depolarizing during high-frequency stimulation. Depolarization in the absence of synaptic activity is not sufficient to produce LTP. Depolarization of the postsynaptic CA1 cell, coupled with minimal stimulation of the axons, produces LTP, indicating that there are two requirements for LTP at this synapse: depolarization and synaptic activity. The axon terminals that synapse

Long-Term Potentiation

Long-term potentiation (LTP) is not a magical property of the hippocampus. Changes in synaptic strength are an emergent property of many synapses, with LTP shown in many neurons throughout the nervous systems of vertebrates and invertebrates, as illustrated in the *Aplysia* sensory-to-motor connections discussed in the previous chapter.

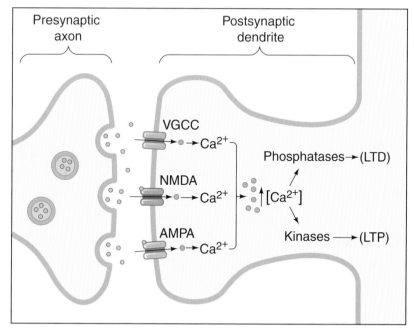

Figure 8.2 Molecular mechanisms of LTP in the hippocampus. This figure shows an axon terminal with a spine on a pyramidal neuron dendrite. High-frequency stimulation of the axon depolarizes the postsynaptic spine to remove the Mg^{2+} block from the NMDA receptor. Ca^{2+} entry via the NMDA as well as AMPA receptors and voltage gated calcium channels (VGCC) combine to elevate Ca^{2+} levels sufficient to activate specific Ca^{2+} dependent protein kinases, including CaMKII. CaMKII activation alters the activity of numerous substrates by phosphorylation to produce LTP.

The Hippocampal Slice Preparation

The *tractability* (ease of study) of long-term potentiation (LTP) in the hippocampal slice preparation was a driving force for its initial popularity as an isolated brain preparation where changes in synaptic plasticity could be easily investigated. For example, LTP can be easily studied using extracellular recordings to monitor changes in the synaptic strength of many neurons, or more sophisticated electrophysiology can be applied (i.e., patch clamp) and individual neurons can be studied as we discussed for simple systems like *Aplysia*.

onto the CA1 pyramidal neurons release glutamate (the major excitatory neurotransmitter in the brain). Glutamate binds to specific receptors on the postsynaptic neuron to produce depolarization. One glutamate receptor subtype, called the AMPA receptor, is distinguished by its ability to bind the compound AMPA and importance in LTP. Recent studies suggest that AMPA receptors can be moved in and out of the membrane in response to neuronal activity. In addition to AMPA receptors, another subtype of glutamate receptor that is important for LTP is the NMDA receptor. The NMDA receptor is distinguished from AMPA receptors by its ability to bind N-methyl-D-aspartate. NMDA receptors do not function to depolarize the membrane, but rather to permit the influx of calcium into the synaptic terminal.

Pharmacological inhibition of NMDA receptors blocks LTP, as does preventing calcium levels from rising in the postsynaptic neuron. Thus, in addition to the high frequency of synaptic activation (which produces a large depolarization and glutamate), LTP also requires NMDA receptor activation and an increase in intracellular calcium. The action of calcium in the postsynaptic cell is quite complex, as there are many proteins that bind calcium directly or bind to proteins that bind calcium. Thus, as we discussed cAMP in Chapter 7, calcium is also considered a second messenger and an increase in intracellular calcium levels functions to activate specific calcium-dependent biochemical responses inside the cell.

THE INDUCTION AND MAINTENANCE OF LTP

The molecular mechanisms responsible for LTP can grouped into different stages: those required to induce or initiate LTP and those required to maintain LTP once it has been produced. The induction of LTP on the CA1 pyramidal neurons has three main requirements: 1) strong synaptic depolarization, 2) NMDA-receptor activation, and 3) the elevation of intracellular calcium. Calcium-dependent processes important for induction of LTP are complex and many protein targets have been identified as necessary for induction of LTP using both genetic and pharmacological methods. One target in particular, calcium/calmodulin-dependent protein kinase II (**CaMKII**), is essential for LTP. It has been shown that when the action of CaMKII is blocked (i.e., through genetic deletion in transgenic animals or by chemical inhibitors), LTP formation is disrupted. The induction period does not require new protein synthesis; maintenance of LTP, however, does. Thus, in an analogous fashion to the short-term and long-term forms of sensitization in *Aplysia*, an increase in synaptic strength can be initiated without new proteins. For this increase to become sustained or long-lasting, however, new proteins are required. Like long-term learning and synaptic plasticity in *Aplysia*, the regulation of protein synthesis is coupled to cAMP elevation and PKA activation during the maintenance phase of LTP. Thus, synaptic plasticity in vertebrates appears to use many of the same molecular mechanisms and molecules seen in invertebrates.

THE ASSOCIATIVE NATURE OF LTP

The relationship between glutamate release by the **axon terminals** (i.e., synaptic activation) and strong depolarization of the CA1 pyramidal neurons in producing NMDA-receptor activation is called associative-LTP. The association of postsynaptic depolarization and synaptic activity has obvious implication for learning theories (see Chapter 3). For associative learning to occur, such as with Pavlov's dogs, a specific temporal pairing is required (in this case, for the tone to be conditioned to represent the presentation of food). In an analogous fashion, LTP can only be produced at the CA1 neurons when the cells are activated at a high enough frequency to permit synaptic activity and postsynaptic depolarization coincidentally. At the molecular level, this association is produced because NMDA-receptor activation is prevented by magnesium, which blocks the receptor and prevents calcium from entering the cell. With high levels of synaptic activity, the postsynaptic cell is depolarized sufficiently to release the magnesium block and permit calcium into the cell through the NMDA receptors. Interestingly, the LTP produced between the axons from the dentate gyrus, which synapse onto the CA3 pyramidal neurons (synapse 2 in Figure 8.1A), is NMDA-independent and presumably nonassociative. It is currently unknown why the circuitry of the hippocampus utilizes multiple forms and mechanisms of LTP.

LTP IS SYNAPSE SPECIFIC

A typical pyramidal cell dendrite makes thousands of synaptic contacts, suggesting that, in principle, each pyramidal cell of the hippocampus (or any neuron in the brain) has the capacity to process and store many bits of information. Thus, a question in the LTP field was whether the synaptic contacts in the same cell could function independently of one another in regard to synaptic plasticity. For example, two different electrodes can effectively stimulate synapses close to the cell body (i.e., proximal) or synapses a long distance from the cell body (i.e., distal). At the axons that terminate on the CA1 pyramidal neurons, researchers must find two distinct groups of axons that converge on a single CA1 pyramidal while maintaining a recording electrode in the CA1 pyramidal cell field or within the cell itself to monitor postsynaptic activity. In such a configuration, distal synapses undergo LTP in response to high frequency stimulation, whereas the synaptic efficacy of the proximal synapses remains unchanged. This indicates that the synapses on the cell can be independently regulated in respect to their synaptic efficacy. This presents a fundamental "sorting" problem at the molecular level, because, as described above, the maintenance phase of LTP requires new proteins. How newly synthesized proteins find the correct synapse or group of synapses to maintain LTP is indeed a mystery.

LTP AND BEHAVIOR

Historically, LTP research began on the belief that changes in synaptic strength were fundamental events in altering neural circuits for learning and memory. Ramón y Cajal first proposed this idea and countless researchers since Bliss and Lomo have made considerable efforts to describe the cellular and molecular mechanisms of LTP without having direct evidence that changes in synaptic strength actually occur with learning. This statement must be confined to vertebrates because Eric Kandel and his colleagues have shown in *Aplysia* that changes in synaptic strength are observed with learning. Thus, one of the quests of neuroscience is to demonstrate that LTP mediates experience-dependent learning in vertebrates and especially mammals.

Using the genetic approach, researchers have demonstrated that transgenic rodents that have been modified to reduce CaMKII levels in the brain do not exhibit hippocampal LTP. These LTP-deficient animals have little capacity for spatial learning tasks. This study suggests that if LTP is blocked in the hippocampus, learning of a hippocampal-targeted task like spatial relationships is also blocked. This evidence is correlative, but it does suggest that LTP may function in vertebrate learning. Researchers are now searching for experimental support for LTP in learning and memory, such as showing that specific synapses in the brain become potentiated after learning. Evidence like this has been difficult to acquire, however, as learning and memory is distributed throughout the brain. The chance of sampling the relevant neurons involved in a specific learned behavior is small (remember, there are roughly a 100 billion neurons in the human brain and 100 trillion synapses). There is evidence that a single exposure to drugs of addiction produces LTP-like changes in specific regions of the brain, a phenomenon that is also dependent upon NMDA receptors. These data are only the beginning in the search to show that changes in synaptic strength underlie experience-dependent changes in an organism's behavior.

■ **Learn more about LTP** Search the Internet for *synaptic plasticity* or *Aplysia*.

9 Strategies to Enhance and Disrupt Learning and Memory

21st CENTURY NEUROSCIENCE—MEDICATING LEARNING AND MEMORY

Animal models have greatly expanded our knowledge about the molecular mechanisms of learning and memory. Research has repeatedly revealed conservation of regulatory proteins (e.g., CaMKII and PKA) and their signaling pathways (e.g., calcium and cAMP) throughout the animal kingdom. Scientists today hope that the many molecular targets discovered in animal models can be exploited to enhance learning and memory in humans. One goal of many pharmaceutical and biotechnology companies is to develop humankind's first "smart pills"—pills that will make you learn faster and remember longer and more clearly. Many companies are also working on medications to help the brain forget. Traumatic experiences associated with war, extreme violence, and mental illness haunt many individuals to the point of causing serious mental distress. Thus, pills to alleviate bad experiences, or "forget pills," may also be on the horizon. In this chapter, we look at a few of the molecular targets that researchers are exploring, as well as potential alternative remedies and how lifestyle can enhance learning and memory.

THE SEARCH FOR DRUGS THAT ENHANCE OR DISRUPT MEMORY

Loss of mental function due to memory loss with aging is projected to become a serious economical and social issue for the United States in the 21st century. Worldwide, the average life span is around 65 years for men and 70 years for women. Also, as the "Baby Boomer" population ages, a larger number of Americans is reaching the age where memory loss occurs. In the last two centuries, the average life span has doubled, increasing steadily at a rate of about 3 months per year, with no indication that this trend is slowing. Thus, the total number of Americans who suffer from memory loss increases with every generation and will continue to increase dramatically, unless science and/or medicine are able to intervene. Loss of mental function with aging is not always indicative of disease. For example, senility is a gradual loss of memory that often occurs with aging. Forgetting the name of an old army buddy or a high school sweetheart when you reach your 60s or 70s is an example of normal aging. The medical community is concerned primarily with stopping dramatic memory loss, such as that associated with Alzheimer's disease, since this process robs a person of his or her life's history and identity. Neuroscientists are working fervently to develop a treatment that could postpone or eradicate Alzheimer's disease (see "Alzheimer's Disease and Senility" box).

One of the strategies employed by Memory Pharmaceuticals in Montvale, New Jersey, is to design new drugs that target the molecular pathways uncovered by Eric Kandel and his colleagues in *Aplysia*, such as drugs that regulate cAMP and calcium-dependent pathways. In 2003, Roche Pharmaceuticals (based in Nutley, New Jersey) selected one candidate, MEM1414, to move into human trials for the treatment of Alzheimer's disease.

Another line of research targets the receptors that nicotine activates in the brain. Nicotine, the addictive component of tobacco, has long been known to enhance mental focus and attention; however, the health risks of smoking and smokeless tobacco preclude the use of tobacco products for promoting memory. Subsequently, researchers are examining MEM3454, a compound that interacts with the nicotine receptor in the brain, being developed by Memory Pharmaceuticals for treatment of Alzheimer's disease. C105, a new molecule manufactured by Providence, Rhode Island–based Sention, is currently being studied in human trials for the treatment of

Alzheimer's Disease and Senility

We have all forgotten a name or common fact in conversation, and perhaps even repeated a story without realizing it. Elderly people and others might perceive holes in their mental fabric as senility; however, slow and gradual missteps in an individual's mental functions are different from the early onset and rapid progression of Alzheimer's disease, which appears as a steep loss of mental capacity, including thought, memory, and language. Alzheimer's disease is named after Dr. Alois Alzheimer, a German physician, who at the turn of the 20th century, reported that a patient with severe mental defects also possessed abnormal clumps and tangles in the nerve fibers of her brain upon autopsy. Today, these *amyloid plaques* and *neurofibrillary tangles*, as they are termed, are central to the diagnosis of Alzheimer's disease. These alterations in brain tissue are what differentiate normal aging from Alzheimer's disease. Researchers have also observed significant neuronal death in the brains of Alzheimer's disease patients, as well as decreased levels of specific neurotransmitters. It is not known if these functional changes relate to the plaques and tangles. Approximately 5 million people in the United States suffer from Alzheimer's memory impairment. The mechanism and actions of this drug have not yet been disclosed to the public; however, the results of these trials are expected to become public in 2006. Cortex Pharmaceuticals, in Orange County, California, along with several other companies, has targeted a class of molecules called ampakines for drug development. These drugs are designed to interact with specific glutamate receptors in the brain and are being developed to enhance neuronal function in children and adults.

disease. The prevalence of Alzheimer's disease in the United States is expected to increase by 27% by the year 2010, with projections of an increase of 70% and 300% by the years 2030 and 2050, respectively. Finding a cure for this looming public health disaster is essential to prevent Alzheimer's disease from overwhelming our healthcare system. Although the cause of Alzheimer's disease is a subject of debate, there is little doubt that both age and genetics are significant risk factors. In addition to examining family history, scientists are exploring the role of diet, education, environment, and mental and social activities on the incidence and development of Alzheimer's disease. Researchers across the globe are racing to identify medications or other interventions that can prevent the onset, slow the progression, and reduce the symptoms of Alzheimer's disease. Currently, the available therapy options are only modestly effective in slowing the progression of the disease's symptoms, particularly among patients in the early or middle stages of the disease. Other medications are used to help control the behavioral symptoms of the disease, such as sleeplessness, agitation, wandering, anxiety, and depression. Effective treatment of the symptoms of Alzheimer's disease can make patients more comfortable and render their care easier for caregivers.

FORGET ABOUT IT!

The concept that forgetting could be beneficial may seem counterintuitive because memory is typically viewed in a positive manner. Not all memories, however, are happy ones. Some people have past experiences that are so painful that remembering them makes it impossible to lead a normal life. For example, post-traumatic stress syndrome is associated with severe mental anguish and stress. This condition is not limited to war and other acts of extreme violence. Any form of human suffering (e.g., car accident, mugging, sudden death of a family member) can lead to such overwhelming mental distress that an individual simply cannot carry out his or her normal day-to-day existence. Flashbacks, guilt, and past emotions become so consuming that individuals who suffer from this condition cannot move on with their lives. Memories formed during unusual circumstances, both highly emotional and stressful, tend to be stronger or more severe relative to other memories. One idea is that stress hormones exaggerate the strength of newly formed memories. This hypothesis was put forward by Dr. Roger K. Pittman at Massachusetts General Hospital. Pittman observed that patients admitted to the hospital after a stressful event were less likely to display post-traumatic stress–like behavior when the drug propranolol was given immediately following their hospital admittance. Propranolol blocks the actions of the stress-related hormones adrenaline and noradrenaline on the brain. Pittman admits that one problem with propranolol is that the drug cannot distinguish between emotionally charged events that are happy and those that are painful. Pittman contends, however, that normal memories established in the absence of emotion should be unaffected. Therefore, this type of a medication is not used to induce global amnesia, but rather to blunt the strength of emotionally charged memories.

ENHANCING LEARNING AND MEMORY WITH ALTERNATIVE REMEDIES

No prescription drugs for enhancing your memory are currently available. There are, however, many over-the-counter products that claim to enhance memory. Alternative remedies to enhance cognitive abilities can be found in most grocery stores, pharmacies, vitamin warehouses, and even gas stations. Most of these products claim to have "natural" memory-enhancing capabilities.

If you search the Internet, you will find many examples of herbal products that are sold to enhance mental capacity. Many of the companies that manufacture these products do not explain how the products' ingredients will supposedly augment learning and memory, nor do they cite clinical evidence of their efficacy. Nevertheless, examples of herbs or compounds that are suspected to "naturally" enhance cognitive abilities can be found all over television and magazine advertising. One substance, acetyl-L-carnitine, is derived from the amino acid L-carnitine. Acetyl-L-carnitine has been implicated in brain function, because it is important for energy synthesis and the formation of neuronal membrane, and because it is similar in structure to an important neurotransmitter in the brain, acetylcholine. Levels of acetyl-L-carnitine appear to decrease with age, and a combination of methionine and lysine supplements might help offset the natural decline in carnitine production. The ginkgo tree is the oldest surviving tree species on the planet and the ginkgo nut has been used in ancient Chinese remedies to treat many ailments associated with mental decline and decreased blood flow. Ginkgo extracts are rich in a type of antioxidant called flavonoids, and may function to increase blood flow to the brain to enhance neuronal activity. Phosphatidyl serine is another example of a cognitive supplement. It is highly enriched in neuronal membranes and, as a phospholipid, it is synthesized by the body. It is generally difficult to obtain phosphatidyl serine through food. Manufacturers of phosphatidyl serine supplements claim that this compound naturally improves the body's ability to repair and maintain neuronal health, and thus enhances mental function.

There are several issues regarding the use of marketed supplements to enhance brain function. The main problem is that "natural" herbal products are not subject to the same standards of efficacy and safety that a pharmaceutical product must pass, through the Food and Drug Administration (FDA), before being approved for use. For example, the amount of active ginkgo extract in the different supplements sold nationwide varies widely from one manufacturer to the next. Thus, even if this agent was able to improve your memory, the relative amount of functional herb may be almost negligible in some of the products. Another problem with herbal medications is the lack of information about potentially dangerous interactions with other drugs. A person who decides to take these compounds should always consult his or her physician or pharmacist before doing so.

A HEALTHY LIFESTYLE AFFECTS LEARNING AND MEMORY

The effects of diet on learning and memory are currently being studied. Health professionals hope that maintaining a balanced diet will prove to be a natural, effective way to recharge and turbo-charge brain function. For example, foods rich in antioxidants are believed to protect the brain from the body's natural tendency to produce free radicals, which are highly reactive molecules that can damage cells. Research led by Dr. Carl Cotman at the University of California, Irvine, demonstrated that old dogs could indeed be taught new tricks: Aging dogs fed antioxidants for several years were able to learn new tasks and also displayed fewer signs of mental degeneration than were seen in the brains of littermates that had not been given antioxidants. Antioxidants are found in many foods besides gingko extracts. One simply has to select the right foods to get the benefits of antioxidants. Purple fruits and vegetables (such as blueberries, cranberries, and red grapes) may be especially beneficial to the brain. Foods rich in B-vitamins (niacin and folic acid)—such as lean meat, fish, legumes, dairy products, and green leafy vegetables—have also been shown to be beneficial to mental function.

A negative contribution of diet on brain function also appears to exist, as diets high in fats or carbohydrates are considered to reduce learning and memory. People in the United States tend to consume diets high in partially hydrogenated vegetable fats and oxidized fats, which clog arteries and reduce blood flow. The brain is one of the organs most sensitive to reduced blood flow, as it depends almost entirely on having access to the oxygen and glucose in blood for its normal metabolism. High-carbohydrate diets can also leave the mind tired and sluggish, possibly due to the reduced glucose content of the blood that tends to follow the initial glucose spike produced by consumption of foods rich in sugar. Regular exercise appears to increase mental function in aging adults, possibly because of its role in maintaining a healthy weight and improving circulation—all of which leads to healthier brains, as revealed by fMRI and behavioral tests.

SLEEP AND LEARNING

Lifestyle changes to enhance learning and memory may include changing one's sleep habits. Do you think you will perform better on a test by cramming all night and forgoing sleep? Many individuals consider sleep a waste of time—a zero-sum game in which you lose precious waking hours. Researchers have shown that brain activity during sleep is far from being switched off, but rather continues throughout much of the night. Brain activity monitoring in sleeping rodents has shown that different areas of the brain produce ripples or waves of activity as they communicate back and forth in specific circuits. In sleeping rodents, the part of the neocortex important for processing sensory information (somatosensory cortex) and the hippocampus appear to communicate back and forth during slow-wave sleep (the longest sleep pattern of the night). Why activate neuronal circuits normally related to acquiring learned behaviors in awake animals? Sleep researchers postulate that new learning and memories are established by the circuits of the brain through a form of subconscious rehearsal while sleeping. Thus, sleep is *not* a waste of the body's time, but rather can be viewed as time when the brain is allowed to unplug from getting new sensory information so that it can process and reprocess the day's events, possibly in an attempt to move the day's important experiences into a longer, more stable form of memory (see "Greasing the Brain's Gears" box).

SUMMARY

As our understanding of the molecular mechanisms of learning and memory has grown, pharmaceutical and biotechnology companies finally have sufficient knowledge to develop products that enhance these processes. Among the possibilities being explored for such products are drugs that improve memory. Paradoxically, research has also been undertaken to develop drugs that help a person forget traumatic or painful experiences—such a product would be helpful in the treatment of post-traumatic stress disorder.

Because people in the United States are living longer, and because memory problems are commonly associated with old age, drugs that improve memory could be of great use—particularly in the treatment of Alzheimer's disease. Several pharmaceutical and biotechnology companies are actively working to develop drugs that influence the molecular pathways of learning and memory. Among the molecular pathways being targeted by re-

Greasing the Brain's Gears

Many neuroscientists view the brain like a muscle: "Use it or lose it!" Brainteasers like crossword and mathematical puzzles can be viewed as gymnastics for your brain. In fact, listening to classical music (e.g., Bach, Beethoven, and Mozart) stimulates brain activity in real time, as shown by fMRI. Exposing your brain to classical music or word and math puzzles are examples of passive mechanisms to improve memory. Active mechanisms and many self-help theories on augmenting learning and memory also abound. Rehearsal, one common method for enhancing learning and memory, involves repeating information in a constructive manner (e.g., vocalizing and/or writing down the information to be learned) in the hope that multiple exposures will move the newly acquired information from short-term memory into long-term memory. When using rehearsal strategies to learn new information, it is important to space the training sessions over time. In other words, start several days before your test. Anyone who has attempted to cram the night before a test knows that this is not an effective way to acquire and remember large amounts of information for extended periods of time. Most memories decay over time, a process that is a natural property of the brain. An ongoing debate in the study of memory is whether we actually ever forget something or whether we simply become unable to retrieve the relevant information (i.e, forgetting is an accessibility problem, not a storage problem). Thus, the next time you cannot remember something that you are certain you knew before, consider whether you have truly forgotten the information, or whether your brain is simply refusing to grant you access to it!

searchers are the cAMP and calcium-dependent pathways, as well as the brain's nicotine and glutamate receptors. Some companies have advanced to the stage of testing potential drugs in human patients, but as of today few if any memory-enhancing (or memory-suppressing) drugs have been brought to the market.

Another area of interest—and possible caution—for consumers is the rapid growth of the alternative remedies market. A large number of so-called natural memory-enhancement agents have been made available as over-the-counter products. U.S. law does not require alternative products to meet any set standard of efficacy or safety, so the claims made by these products are usually unsubstantiated. Of more concern, the ingredients in these products may not be pure or even listed on the label. Also, some "natural" products can produce dangerous effects when they are taken with certain prescription drugs—a warning not required and rarely mentioned on the labels of these over-the-counter agents. Some of the "natural" memory-enhancement products available today include ginkgo, phosphatidyl serine, and acetyl-L-carnitine.

Investigations into the effect of diet and exercise on learning and memory is ongoing. Foods rich in antioxidants are believed to protect against the brain damage that occurs with aging through the action of molecules called free radicals. B vitamins are also thought to be beneficial to mental function. Diets containing high levels of fats and carbohydrates are believed to have a negative effect on memory. Exercise, on the other hand, is believed to increase mental function. Finally, the importance of sleep to the memory formation process has been established by researchers.

■ **Learn more about memory enhancement** Search the Internet for *diet and memory*, *sleep and memory*, or *music and memory*.

Glossary

Action potential A change in the electrochemical balance between the inside and outside of a neuron.

Adenylyl cyclase A protein that increases levels of the second messenger cAMP within a cell.

Alzheimer's disease A degenerative disease of the brain characterized by confusion, disorientation, memory loss, speech disturbances, and a progressive loss of overall mental capacity.

Amino acid Any of a class of 20 molecules that combine to form proteins in living organisms.

Amygdala A structure in the vertebrate brain that is involved in the generation of emotion and the development of memories.

Anterograde amnesia Loss of memory for events that follow an injury to the brain.

Associative learning A change in an animal's behavior that reflects recognition of an initially neutral stimulus from its association with a meaningful stimulus; an example of classical condition or Pavlovian learning.

Autonomic Occurring without conscious effort.

Axon Projection that functions to transmit information to other neurons or excitable cell (e.g., muscle).

Behaviorism The study of measurable and observable events to explain human behavior and the acquisition of knowledge.

CaMKII The multifunctional Ca^{2+}/calmodulin-dependent protein kinase is activated by the Ca^{2+} binding protein calmodulin, and alters the activity or location of specific substrates in the cell by phosphorylation to alter cell function.

cAMP Cyclic nucleotide of adenosine, a second messenger that activates a multifunctional protein kinase, or PKA.

Cell body The main structure of a neuron.

Central nervous system The brain and spinal cord.

Cerebral cortex The outer layer of the cerebral hemispheres that is responsible for higher brain functions, including sensation, movement, thought, and memory.

Cerebral hemispheres The two large symmetrical lobes that make up the majority of the brain.

Cerebrospinal fluid The fluid that cushions the brain and removes waste products from both the brain and spinal cord.

Chunking Any process that results in extending short-term memory by attempting to recode the smaller bits of information into large screens.

Classical conditioning A form of associative learning in which there is no relationship between the response and reinforcer; requires forming new associations between two stimuli that initially had no connection.

Cognitive neuroscience The branch of neuroscience dedicated to understanding how the brain thinks.

Cognitivism The psychological approach believing that human behavior or acquisition of knowledge must consider key elements of mental function such as perception, learning, and thought.

Conditioned response In classical conditioning, the response that an organism learns to make.

Conditioned stimulus A neutral stimulus that initially has no instructive quality, yet becomes conditioned to represent the unconditioned stimulus.

Confabulation The unconscious act of filling in the gaps of a memory with information or details that eventually become indistinguishable from the actual details of the memory.

Consolidation The movement of information from short-term to long-term memory.

Correlative approach A research strategy used to identify changes in the content and distribution of proteins associated with specific physiological or pathological functions.

DAG Diacylglycerol, a second messenger that activates a multifunctional protein kinase, protein kinase C.

Declarative memory Memories of facts and events.

Delayed matching-to-sample task A paradigm where a test subject must wait until after the presentation of an object to respond, the correct response being rejection of the novel object.

Delayed nonmatching-to-sample task A paradigm where a test subject must wait until after the presentation of an object to respond, the correct response being selection of a novel object.

Dendrite The branch-like part of a neuron that receives information, or input, from the environment and other neurons.

Dephosphorylation An enzymatic activity carried out by protein phosphatases to reverse the action of substrate phosphorylation by protein kinases.

Depolarization Movement of a membrane potential in the positive direction.

Dishabituating When a sensitizing stimulus reverses a habituating stimulus.

Distributed learning Storage of information in memory over a long period of time rather than all at once.

Echoic memory Representation of aural (hearing-related) stimulus and one mode of sensory memories.

Eidetic imagery The ability to recall images, sounds, or objects with amazing accuracy and seemingly unlimited capacity.

Electrophysiology Electrical recording techniques that allow researchers to measure very small changes in electric current across cell membranes.

Empiricism A philosophical view that maintains that true knowledge can only result from experience and the senses.

Episodic memory A component of declarative memory that refers to events in one's life; memories and events linked to the past.

Eukaryote Any organism made up of cells that have a membrane-enclosed nucleus and other cell compartments.

Excitable Able to respond to stimuli.

Explicit memory Memories of specific events that require conscious recollection.

Extinction The loss of a conditioned response as it is continuously applied in the absence of the unconditioned stimulus.

Forward genetics The process of altering an organism's genome to find specific genes that create a phenotype of interest (i.e., classical genetics).

Frontal lobe The region of cortex behind the forehead that makes up the majority of the cerebral hemispheres, important for reasoning, planning, attention, and language.

Functional magnetic resonance imaging (fMRI) A technique that permits researchers to view changes in oxygen levels in the brain for use as an index of neuronal activity.

Ganglion A collection or grouping of nerve cells (plural is *ganglia*).

Genetic screen A procedure to test for individuals that possess a phenotype of interest.

Genome All of the genetic material (genes) that make up an organism.

Granule cell A type of neuron associated with the cerebellum and cerebrum.

Gyri The prominent convoluted bumps on the surface of the cerebral hemispheres (singular is *gyrus*).

Habituation A decrease in the behavioral response to a repeated non-noxious stimulus.

Haptic memory Representation of touch stimulus; one mode of sensory memory.

High-throughput approaches Research approaches that are specifically designed to utilize very small amounts of biological material and require very little manipulation so that many samples may be analyzed at once.

Hippocampus Structure in the brain that plays a crucial role in establishing long-term memories; part of the limbic system.

Hydrolyzation Process in which a material is broken down through a reaction with water.

Hypothalamus A structure in the brain involved in autonomic processes and believed to be important in controlling sleep and wakefulness; part of the limbic system.

Iconic memory Representation of a visual stimulus; one mode of sensory memory.

Immediate memory The memory formed immediately after encountering a stimulus.

Implicit memory Memories associated with events or tasks that cannot be consciously recalled; they can either be performed or not, like reading or riding a bicycle.

Incidental learning A form of complex learning in higher mammals, especially primates, that occurs in the absence of any identifiable associated event, utilizing perception and insight to generate solutions to situations that were previously unsolvable.

Inducible knockout The ability to produce gene disruption in an organism's genome with specific temporal and spatial control.

Innervate To supply with nerves.

Instrumental conditioning A form of associative learning whereby learning is done to obtain a reward or avoid punishment; however, the nature of the response is not fixed, but rather discovered by the subject.

Interneurons Neurons that function to modulate a behavior by regulating the input-output properties of other neurons in a functional circuit.

Korsakoff's syndrome Memory loss that results from vitamin B deficiency.

Law of Contiguity Law stating that either of two events that occur together in space and time can be recalled to memory upon subsequent exposure to the other event.

Learning The process of acquiring skill or knowledge.

Learning curve A measure of learning relative to the amount of practice.

Lesion A wound or injury that damages tissue.

Limbic system A group of brain structures common to all mammals that play a role in motivation, emotion, olfaction, behavior, memory, and learning.

Long-term depression (LTD) A long-lasting decrease in the synaptic connectivity between neurons produced by specific biochemical changes related to calcium signaling.

Long-term memory A phase of memory in which information or a stimulus is stored for periods that may approach the lifetime of an organism.

Long-term potentiation (LTP) A long-lasting increase in the synaptic connectivity between neurons produced by specific biochemical changes related to calcium signaling.

Mechanical memory A region of memory concerned with the formation of skills and habits.

Membrane potential The difference in electrical voltage between the inside and outside of a cell.

Memory The ability to recall past experience or information.

Memory engram The cellular representation or substrate of memory.

Meninges Tissue on top of the brain that functions to pad and protect the nervous system; consists of three layers: the dura mater, pia mater, and the space between these two tissues, the arachnoid space.

Mirror tracing A learning and memory task used to evaluate procedural memory skills by requiring a test subject to read or draw backward.

Mnemonic device A creative strategy used to aid memory.

Motor neurons Neurons in the central nervous system that convey information to effector tissues, such as muscles and glands.

Mutation A change in an organism's genetic information.

Nervous system The cells, tissues, and organs that regulate an organism's responses to internal and external stimuli.

Neuron A nerve cell that consists of a cell body, dendrites, and an axon.

Neuronal network A subsystem of the brain that is formed by functionally related neurons.

Neuroscience Branch of science concerned with the growth, development, and function of the nervous system.

Neurotransmission The exchange of chemical messengers, termed neurotransmitters, at the synapse between communicating neurons.

Neurotransmitter A chemical messenger involved in the communication between neurons.

Nonassociative learning The change in an animal's behavior toward a stimulus without an apparent association; habituation and sensitization are the major forms of this primitive type of learning.

Occipital lobe The region of the cerebral cortex important for processing visual information, situated at the back of the cerebral hemispheres.

Olfactory Relating to the sense of smell.

Operant conditioning A process of behavioral modification in which the frequency of a specific behavior is increased or decreased by positive or negative reinforcement each time the behavior is exhibited.

Parietal lobe The region of the cerebral cortex important for sensory processing, including pain, temperature, touch, and pressure, as well as spatial orientation and speech and language development.

Pavlovian conditioning Classical conditioning.

Peripheral nervous system The nervous system outside of the brain and cord; consists of cranial and spinal nerves and the sympathetic and parasympathetic nervous systems.

Phenotype The observable behavioral or biochemical characteristics of an organism as determined by how its genetic makeup interacts with the environment.

Phosphatases Proteins that counter the action of kinases by reversing phosphorylation.

Phosphodiesterases Proteins that reduce cAMP levels inside cells.

Phosphorylation A posttranslational modification on the substrates of protein kinases that alters the proteins' localization or activity.

Phrenology The theory that human skull size, shape, and contours can be used to describe personality and intellectual capacity.

PKA The multifunctional protein kinase A is activated by increased cAMP levels inside the cell. Active PKA functions to regulate the activity or location of specific substrates via a rapid and specific process, termed phosphorylation.

PKC The multifunctional protein kinase C is activated by increased DAG levels inside the cell. Active PKC functions to regulate the activity or location of specific substrates via a rapid and specific process, termed phosphorylation.

Plasticity The capacity of a biological process to be continuously sculpted, modified, or regulated.

Post-traumatic stress disorder A psychiatric illness that sometimes occurs after a person experiences a severely traumatic event.

Priming The act of presenting elements of a stimulus in an attempt to facilitate remembering what the stimulus or event actually was.

Procedural memory A long-term memory of a process or procedure; refers to "how-to" knowledge.

Protein Molecules made up of amino acids that are essential for the growth and repair of the body's tissues and that provide energy, act as enzymes, and control cellular chemical reactions.

Proteomics The study of all the proteins in an organism's genome in regard to their specific physiological or pathological functions.

Pyramidal neuron A type of nerve cell in the cerebral cortex.

Rationalism A philosophical view stating that reason itself forms the basis of knowledge.

Reason The ability to think, make inferences, and draw conclusions.

Recall The process of remembering.

Refabrication The unconscious act of filling in the gaps of a memory without being able to later distinguish reality from fabrication.

Representative memory A region of memory concerned with the recollection of ideas and events.

Retention An ability to recall information that has been learned or experienced.

Retrograde amnesia A form of memory loss in which a person is unable to remember events that occurred before a brain injury.

Reverse genetics The process of deleting or adding a specific gene to an organism's genome to ascertain the function of the gene at the molecular, cellular, and behavioral level.

Rote A memorizing process that uses routine or repetition.

Scientific method A method whereby scientists attempt to construct a consistent, reliable, and nonarbitrary representation of the world. The four steps include 1) description of a phenomenon, 2) generation of a hypothesis to explain the phenomenon, 3) use of the hypothesis to predict the existence of other phenomena related to the process being studied, and 4) experimentation to prove or disprove the hypothesis by independent means.

Second messengers Small molecules that link extracellular signals with specific biochemical pathways inside cells.

Semantic memory A component of declarative memory referring to the memories that are not specific to an individual's life.

Senility The mental deterioration associated with aging.

Sensitive memory A region of memory concerned with emotions and feelings.

Sensitization The increasing of the strength of a reflexive response produced by the presentation of a noxious stimulus.

Sensory memory The memory of a sensory stimulus after the event has passed; there are five modalities: touch, taste, hearing, vision, and smell.

Sensory neurons Specialized neurons within the nervous system that convert external stimuli (e.g., heat, cold, touch) into neuronal activity, as well as the neurons that pass and integrate the external stimuli within the nervous system.

Sensory stimuli Any of the five stimuli that neurons have evolved to react to, including touch, vision, hearing, smell, and taste.

Short-term memory A phase of memory in which information or a stimulus is only stored for a brief time.

Skinner box A light- and sound-proof cage or box that usually only has a bar or lever that an animal must learn to press in order to get food or avoid punishment (e.g., shock), originally designed by B. F. Skinner to train birds and rodents.

Soma The central part or cell body of a neuron that contains the nucleus.

Sulci Any of the recessed areas or grooves on the surface of the cerebral hemispheres that lie between gyri (singular is *sulcus*).

Synapse The functional connection between a neuron axon, and another cell.

Synaptic plasticity The potential for synaptic connections to be strengthened or weakened by different patterns of neuronal activity.

Temporal lobe The region of the cerebral cortex important for processing auditory information as well as integrating all sensory information and declarative memory.

Thalamus A structure in the brain that relays impulses from the sensory nerves; part of the limbic system.

Transgenic An organism whose genome has been altered via gene deletion or gene addition.

Unconditioned response A response that is unlearned and automatic.

Unconditioned stimulus A recognizable stimulus that produces an immediate behavioral response.

Ventricle One of the four small cavities or chambers of the brain.

Vertebrate An animal that has a backbone.

Wechsler Memory Scale A test that uses visual and auditory stimuli to evaluate learning, memory, and working memory.

Whole-cell recording Electrical recording technique that allows researchers to measure very small changes in electric current across cell membranes; also known as patch clamping.

Withdrawal reflex A simple neuronal circuit that processes messages without the direct intervention of the brain.

Working memory Short-term memory.

Bibliography

Altenmuller, E. O. "Music in Your Head." *Scientific American Mind* 14(2004): 24–32.

Carmichael, M. "Medicine's Next Level." *Newsweek* (December 6, 2004): 45–50.

Cialdini, R. B. "The Science of Persuasion." *Scientific American Mind* 14(2004): 70–78.

Dudai, Y. *The Neurobiology of Memory: Concepts, Findings, Trends.* New York: Oxford University Press, 1989.

Eichenbaum, H. "Hippocampus: Cognitive Processes and Neural Representations That Underlie Declarative Memory." *Neuron* 44(2004): 5–21.

Gorman, C. "Why We Sleep." *Time* (December 20, 2004): 46–59.

Hitier, R., F. Petit, and T. Préat. "Memories of a Fly." *Scientific American Mind* 14(2004): 78–86.

Illing, R.-B. "Humbled by History." *Scientific American Mind* 14(2004): 86–93.

Javitt, D. C., and J. T. Coyle. "Decoding Schizophrenia." *Scientific American* 290(2004): 48–56.

Levitan, I. B., and L. K. Kaczmarek. *The Neuron: Cell and Molecular Biology.* New York: Oxford University Press, 1997.

Malenka, R. C., and M. F. Bear. "LTP and LTD: An Embarrassment of Riches." *Neuron* 44 (2004): 5–21.

Pauen, M. "Does Free Will Arise Freely?" *Scientific American Mind* 14(2004): 40–48.

Roth, G. "The Quest to Find Consciousness." *Scientific American Mind* 14(2004): 32–40.

Treffert, D. A., and G. L. Wallace. "Islands of Genius." *Scientific American Mind* 14(2004): 14–24.

Vaas, R. "Fear Not." *Scientific American Mind* 14(2004): 62–70.

Further Reading

Kandel, E. R., J. H. Schwartz, and T. H. Jessell. *Principles of Neural Science.* 4th edition. McGraw Hill, 2000.

Roberts, J., and J. Byrne. *From Molecules to Networks: An Introduction to Cellular and Molecular Neuroscience.* Academic Press, 2003.

Yadin, D. *The Neurobiology of Learning and Memory: Concepts, Findings, Truths.* Oxford University Press, 1989.

Websites

Amnesia
http://serendip.brynmawr.edu/bb/neuro/neuro01/web1/Choi.html

Ancient Egypt Medicine
http://www.reshafim.org.il/ad/egypt/timelines/topics/medicine.htm

Animal Learning
http://www.pigeon.psy.tufts.edu/psych26/default.htm

Animal Learning Videos
http://go.owu.edu/;deswartz/introduction.html

Audition and Emotion
http://brain.web-us.com/binaural.htm

Brain Facts
http://faculty.washington.edu/chudler/facts.html

Brain Stuff
http://ifcsun1.ifisiol.unam.mx/Brain/segunda.htm

Children with Amnesia
http://brain.web-us.com/binaural.htm

Cognitivism versus Behaviorism in Learning
http://www.personal.psu.edu/users/t/x/txl166/kb/theory/compar.html

Comparing Brains
http://serendip.brynmawr.edu/bb/kinser/Home1.html

Computing and the Brain
http://www.cs.stir.ac.uk/courses/31YF/Notes/CBnotes.html

Drosophila Names
http://tinman.vetmed.helsinki.fi/eng/drosophila.html

General Definitions for Learning and Memory
http://www.memory-key.com/MemoryGuide/glossary_brain.htm

Genetics of Learning and memory
http://www.ncbi.nlm.nih.gov/books/bv.fcgi?rid5neurosci.box.1701

Hippocampus and LTP
http://www.bris.ac.uk/Depts/Synaptic/info/pathway/hippocampal.htm#MF

History of Neuroscience
  http://faculty.washington.edu/chudler/hist.html

H. M.
  http://www.brainconnection.com/topics/?main5fa/hm-memory

Hodgkin and Huxley's Action Potential
  http://www.stanford.edu/;afodor/HHModel.htm

Intelligence—Brain versus Body Size
  http://serendip.brynmawr.edu/bb/kinser/Size3.html

The Language of Neurons
  http://www.bris.ac.uk/synaptic/public/basics_ch1_2.html

Limbic System
  http://www.ship.edu/;cgboeree/limbicsystem.html
  http://www.driesen.com/brain_view_-_7.htm
  http://www.brainplace.com/bp/brainsystem/limbic.asp

Neuro-Images
  http://www.blackwellpublishing.com/matthews/animate.html
  http://www.blackwellpublishing.com/matthews/figures.html

Pavlov
  http://nobelprize.org/medicine/educational/pavlov/readmore.html

Photographic Memory
  http://pages.slc.edu/;ebj/memory04/questions-answers/
  photographic.htm

Post-traumatic Brain Syndrome
  http://www.uphs.upenn.edu/tbilab/recognition/

Procedural Memory
  http://ahsmail.uwaterloo.ca/kin356/ltm/procedural.htm

Protein Facts
  http://www.friedli.com/herbs/phytochem/proteins.html
  http://www.postmodern.com/;jka/rnaworld/nfrna/nf-rnadefed.html

Sensory Memory
  http://library.thinkquest.org/;C0110291/basic/brain/sensory.php

Smith Papyrus
http://www.neurosurgery.org/cybermuseum/pre20th/epapyrus.html

Structure of Memory
http://ist-socrates.berkeley.edu/;kihlstrm/rmpa00.htm
http://ess.ntu.ac.uk/miller/cognitive/stores.htm
http://www.benbest.com/science/anatmind/anatmd3.html
http://plato.stanford.edu/entries/memory/

Timeline of Neuroscience
http://faculty.washington.edu/chudler/hist.html

Tower of Hanoi
http://www.convict.lu/Jeunes/Hanoi/Tower_of_Hanoi.htm
http://www.lilgames.com/hanoi.shtm

Index

About the Author

Dr. Andy Hudmon received his Bachelor's degree in marine biology and his Master's degree in interdisciplinary physiology under James Sartin at Auburn University in Auburn, Alabama. He earned his Ph.D. in neuroscience under Neal Waxham at The University of Texas Health Science Center in Houston, Texas. He trained as a postdoctoral fellow in the Department of Neurobiology and Anatomy at Stanford University under Howard Schulman, and currently he is an Associate Research Scientist in the Department of Neurology at the Yale University School of Medicine. His current research focuses on delineating the mechanisms of sodium channel regulation and function by protein–protein interactions and phosphorylation.

Picture Credits

Cylert® is a registered trademark of Abbott Laboratories; Trivial Pursuit® is a registered trademark of Horn Abbot Ltd.